D1550651

BEST REGARDS

John McKann

LEAN AGAINST THE WIND

Also by James McKarns

Ten Great Men of the Old Testament
Go Tell Everyone
Seldom Told Bible Tales
Give Us This Day (3 Vols.)

Visit our web site at
www.albahouse.org
(for orders www.alba-house.com)

or call 1-800-343-2522 (ALBA)
and request current catalog

Lean against the Wind

How to Face the Future

JAMES McKARNS

ST PAULS

Alba
House

Library of Congress Cataloging-in-Publication Data

McKarns, James E.
  Lean against the wind: how to face the future / James McKarns.
      p.   cm.
    ISBN 0-8189-0690-1
    1. Success. 2. Conduct of life. I. Title.
  BJ1611.2.M38   1994
  170'.44 — dc20   93-41498
                                                          CIP

Produced and designed in the United States of America by the
Fathers and Brothers of the Society of St. Paul,
2187 Victory Boulevard, Staten Island, New York 10314-6603,
as part of their communications apostolate.

ISBN: 0-8189-0690-1

Printing Information:

Current Printing - first digit   4   5   6   7   8   9   10

Year of Current Printing - first year shown

              2006   2007   2008   2009   2010   2011   2012

"And when the heart is on fire, the imagination is quickened. We dare to dream dreams we never thought possible and to venture down roads largely unexplored."

Diarmuid O'Murchu
Quantum Theology

CONTENTS

PREFACE

One November day, when I was 28 years old, I had come home to visit my parents on the family farm. After dinner dad went into town on some business and mom and I remained sitting at the kitchen table.

During our conversation, we were startled when a gusty east wind suddenly rattled the doors and windows. It howled angrily around the house and yard, swirling dust and small twigs about in its fury. "My lands!" mom exclaimed. It was her favorite expression of surprise.

The chickens ran for cover and the barren pear tree swayed. The forceful wind pushed the three electric lines connecting the house and barn into the shape of a taut half-moon.

My mother grew silent and I waited for her to speak. After a few reflective moments, she said quietly: "That sudden gust of wind reminds me of an incident — when you were a baby." Her words were more a reflection than conversation. The incident she remembered and related to me that evening increased my appreciation for my loving mother.

"It was a very cold winter day," she said. "Donald (my father) and I had just returned from the grocery store. You were only a few months old and we had taken you with us. I got out of the car before he drove into the outside garage and was carrying you into the house." She lingered a bit, then added, "Well, as I walked around the corner of the house a very violent wind hit me in the face. I was caught off guard. The wind came with an upward swooping motion and almost pulled you right out of my arms."

My mother's left arm had been broken in an accident, when she was in college, and remained slightly bent and weakened. "I clung to you with my right arm," she said, "and held on for dear life, but it really frightened me." My mom gave me a little pat on the shoulder and added, "It took all my strength and determination to hold you and reach the porch door. I had to lean against the wind." It was a tender moment and I gave her a hug and thanked her for protecting me.

Since that time I've often thought what my fate might have been had that treacherous wind pulled me from her arms. The concrete blocks and frozen ground would have been a hard and dangerous landing for a three-month-old baby. I could have sustained a serious injury, perhaps a permanent one. The strength of my mother's arms was tested that day and she proved stronger than the unpredictable forces of nature. Often, I have breathed a prayer of gratitude that she kept her balance, held me from falling, and did, indeed, lean against the wind.

There are all kinds of forces and pressures — physical, social, economic and psychological — in our world today that can push us over, throw us back and leave us injured. It's unrealistic to think we can escape all disasters, ills and failures; but many we can. It's within our power to turn apparent defeats into victories and achieve amazing results, if only we are willing to lean against the wind.

Precious gifts of life, health, intelligence and grace have been entrusted to our care. It's frightening to think how quickly and completely they can be snatched from us. They are preserved and developed only with continual effort. Sadly, some do not make that effort.

This book is written to help people face those would-be conquering forces, triumph over them and savor the victories. Its stories and insights are meant to give encouragement.

Over the past 40 years I have made it a point to methodically record inspiring ideas which I've come across. Some I heard and read; others came out of my own experience and, in that sense, are original. That data is now blended into my own personal philosophy of life.

Our particular culture, folklore and homespun philosophy are common property like the air we breathe, the space we occupy and the world we inhabit. Someone once said that there are few original ideas. Most of the stories which come to us are soon passed along to others. Sometimes, we reshape them and add a touch of local color.

I hope this book will stimulate your thought, strengthen your courage and uplift your life. Mostly, may it lead you to find inner peace and be on good terms with others. Perhaps it will also encourage you to share meaningful happenings in your life and family.

What you desire to become or accomplish in life may well be very difficult. But if it is possible, be convinced you can do it — provided you're willing to lean against the wind.

1

PAINT YOUR OWN PORTRAIT

The story is told of a traveling portrait painter who stopped at a small town hoping to find some work. One of those who sat in his chair was a homeless alcoholic. In spite of his dirty unshaven face and bedraggled clothes, he posed with all the dignity he possessed.

After the artist had labored longer than usual, he lifted the portrait from his easel and presented it to his client. The man studied the well-dressed, respectable looking person in the painting and slurred, "That ain't me." The artist who had perceived an inner dignity beneath the man's uncouth exterior promptly replied, "But it is the man you could be."

If you are not the kind of person you want to be, know you can always change for the better. In fact, others may see in you many fine qualities which you can't recognize in yourself. The man in the chair could perceive little goodness or beauty within himself. He saw only weaknesses and broken promises. Others had reinforced his negative image by their cruel words and disgusted glances.

1

You may be struggling with a poor self-image. When you see impressive-looking people and hear their stories of success, are you convinced such accomplishments and honors will never be yours? Maybe you have felt short-changed from childhood. You never really had a fair chance to prove yourself. Perhaps serious problems or setbacks occurred in your later formative years. You might possess a litany of laments, all of which begin with the words: "If only." If only I had been blessed with more understanding parents. If only my family had not been poor. If only I could have attended a better school. If only I were taller or heavier or thinner. If only my nose were smaller, my muscles bigger, my personality better.

Our hurts may be so numerous and monumental that, before we begin listing them, we expect to hear a drum roll. Problems which impair us can be physical, mental, emotional or social. Perhaps they've always plagued us and we feel like born losers, cruelly condemned to a life of misery. We may consider ourselves incapable of finding happiness or success at any job, at any age. That certainly is not the true picture. Regardless of how low, miserable, far-out or fouled up we may be or think we are, it's always possible to be a better person.

Psychologists say that the child we once were still lives within us as adults. We have those same hopes, feelings and fears. We need to recognize the child within. Memories of the past can enlighten the present and guide us to paint a hope-filled but realistic portrait of ourselves for the future.

Our hurts may have come in the form of physical violence, sexual abuse, peer intimidation, or social rejection. Others, perhaps, were better looking, stronger, got higher grades and had more money. We carry all those images with us into adult life. These wounds may have festered in us throughout our formative years but we did survive them. Now, through the supporting help of others and maybe even a bit of counseling, we can change our attitudes and start down a new road. A little prayer speaks to the point: "O God, give me the strength to change what I can, the patience to accept what I can't, and the wisdom to know the difference."

You may be working for a higher position and someone else is promoted. What can you do? Spend the rest of your life crying? Forget it. Go after another. It may provide many more opportunities than the original which you thought you had to have. The greater advantages often are not seen immediately.

Don't lay back waiting for opportunities to come your way. They don't. You have to move out, search and work for them. Some say that hard work produces success, while others claim that luck alone is responsible. The fact is, those who work the hardest are usually the luckiest. Consistent work separates the winner from the wisher. We must accept the flow of life and forge ahead amidst difficulties, rather than retreat within ourselves and hope for luck.

There are people in your life, hopefully many, who love and care for you. These are intelligent individuals and they see the goodness within you. When they say you can do better, be more productive and achieve success, believe them. You, no doubt, see many strengths and abilities in others who don't see them within themselves. Understand that the very same principle applies in your case. In order to improve, it's essential to see clearly where you are at present and where you want to go. Don't expect to be enshrined on Mount Rushmore — there's no room. But set your goals just as high. If your objective is unclear, chances are you will not arrive.

It's very helpful to commit your ideas and plans to paper. There you can dream and detail your own success story. Journaling helps many to be more definite in looking ahead, and keeps a record of where they've been. It's only natural, I know, to want to avoid these probing, concrete sessions in realism for they can be demanding and sometimes painful; yet if you don't, you risk stumbling along like a wounded warrior.

The old story of the eagle egg is applicable here. An eagle egg was placed, to be hatched, with the hen eggs and the baby eagle was raised with the chickens. This eagle never soared above the mountain peaks into the heavens, because it always thought it was a chicken. It spent its whole life scratching in the dirt, its wonderful, natural ability never used.

In 1907 a man died at the age of 48. His

name was Francis Thompson. The world still re-
members him as a brilliant poet. When Francis
was a boy he considered entering the priesthood
but laziness and indifference kept him from the
seminary. He enrolled in medical school and that,
too, proved fruitless. Soon he was addicted to
opium which nearly wrecked both mind and
body. He became a beggar in the slums, making
a little money shining shoes and selling matches.
Finally, through the assistance of a young lady,
Francis was introduced to some people who recognized his rare talent and inner goodness. They
helped him improve his life. In his few remain-
ing years, he wrote some of the best known reli-
gious poetry in the English language.

Thompson saw himself of little account. He
says he ran from God and people and commitments before he was finally compelled to turn
around and face reality. He found fulfillment
when he learned to lean against the wind. His
world famous poem, "The Hound of Heaven," is
a reflection of his own life of running scared.

What a shame, we might say, that Francis
Thompson didn't get his act together sooner. Yet,
the point is, he did recover. And the delicate poetry which lived within him throughout those
long slum years survived, waiting to be released
to the world. It had to be discovered by another.
That's why we need to listen to those who know
us best. They can inspire us to believe in ourselves. Once we are convinced of our own self
worth, accomplishments may not be far behind.

In a town where I once lived, I would often

see the local cable television truck making its service calls. Painted on both sides in large letters were the words: "Seeing Is Believing." That's a fine advertisement for cable TV but it's not a good directive for decision making. Actually seeing is not believing. Seeing is seeing. If you see something then belief has been cancelled out. Believing is not seeing but still trusting it's true. We don't see the unfolded future, but believe it will develop or we can make it happen.

Positive-minded people are convinced they have a better future ahead of them. The envisioned happenings are so clearly fixed in their minds they can "see" them as already fulfilled. In their case "believing is seeing." We, too, can believe so strongly in a future accomplishment that we can see it already present. When our goal is that clearly defined, we're on our way. We may start a million dollars short of being a millionaire but we must begin somewhere.

I have seen countless examples in sports, especially in track and field, where athletes had a dream and then became convinced the dream could be realized. That confident assurance became the motivating power behind their untold hours of practice and eventual victory.

The high-jumpers and pole-vaulters meticulously plot their every move. They dash down the runway, twist, turn, and strain every muscle, clear the bar and land triumphantly in the arms of the soft padding. They've cleared the almost impossible height without even jumping. It was all accomplished in their minds, at the head of the runway, before they ever took the first step. It absolutely must first be seen and achieved in the mind, otherwise the body will never do it. Yet the actual achievement of the strenuous feat does not follow immediately. Between the vision and the victory are those agonizing hours and days of training. One Kenyan marathon runner was quoted, "The will to win means nothing if you don't have the will to prepare."

What is said of athletes is true for all people in every task, profession or endeavor. I've heard it said that the single most important word in the English language is "Attitude." It has a profound bearing on who we are and what we do. How we see ourselves is an absolutely fundamental element in our lives; everything else is shaped by that. The famous country-western singer, Bill Monroe, told a TV audience that he received a tremendous confidence-boost when his boss said, "Bill, if you ever leave here, it will be because you fired yourself." How often have we done exactly that? We've fired ourselves.

I feel sorry for the depressed 58-year-old woman who was asked how things were going for her. Replying in a very negative tone she said: "I'm too young for medicare and too old for men to care." For medicare O.K. For men to care — no way. It's all in the attitude. We can be loved and lovable, but first we must shed that negative attitude about ourselves. I've never heard of there being a certain age beyond which a person is no longer lovable. True, we live in a youth-oriented society, but there is a unique beauty and gracefulness in a person at any age. Someone told me when he turned 50 he stopped looking for the fountain of youth. Now he's looking for the fountain of middle age. That's a healthy attitude. It's realistic. It's wonderful. Malcolm Forbes died in 1990 at the age of 70. He was buried in the Fiji Islands. The epitaph on his tomb reads: "While alive, he lived." I know he was rich, but aren't we all in so many ways?

It is a fallacy of our times to think of richness only in terms of money. Richness can mean a hundred different things and money is only one of them. Having a life to live, friends, freedom from severe pain, an attitude of self-worth and a sense of some accomplishment makes for a unique richness. When we want these possessions and don't have them, then we are poor, even if we have a lot of money.

What do you want? How would you like to see your portrait painted? The dream must precede the reality. Who can forget Dr. Martin Luther King Jr.'s famous, "I Have A Dream" speech? On that memorable day in our Nation's capital, he voiced a tremendous challenge. It was not only a dream for himself but a dream for the well-being of the entire nation.

Refuse to be content with merely browsing through life. Ask those who know and love you, what they see in you. Decide what's realistic and never say, "That ain't me." Paint an attractive picture of yourself by envisioning what is possible. Then be willing to exert the effort to make it all come true.

2

EVERY ROAD
IS NOT AN INTERSTATE

American ingenuity has admirably cut through the mountains and bridged the rivers with thousands of smooth multi-lane highways. These roads display the familiar red, white and blue signs which are welcomed by the traveler. The interstate road system gives assurance to the driver that the miles will pass quickly and with minimal driving effort.

This well-planned cross-country network was promoted by President Eisenhower, basically for military purposes. On these roads troops could move quickly in any direction without facing traffic jams along the way.

Today we take wide smooth highways for granted. They total over 50,000 miles across the United States. The former "major highways" by contrast were mainly two lanes with many curves. They ran through the middle of small towns and big cities. Journeys then were more challenging and much slower. Incidentally, these two-lane highways also generated untold family fights between the driver and the one interpreting the road map. It was easy to miss a turn-off or misinterpret a sign and become lost. Today, the interstates give us clear signs far in advance. Before the advent of the automobile, many of the old roads were primitive paths, often nameless and filled with hazards.

Personal achievement and character development has not and can not match the fast pace of modern day travel. Human accomplishments do not flow in the easy, ordered fashion which we experience on the interstate. The speed and ease with which we travel to success and personal fulfillment is dictated by a different road. Our progress is still slow and often difficult. We want to be further advanced and may even get discouraged. The hazards often appear insurmountable for here we must still travel those primitive roads. But we can take heart because at least we're on our way.

Within the human heart we have our ups and downs, our setbacks and disappointments. Our pace is more akin to traveling Lombard Street in San Francisco — 5 miles per hour and constantly turning. Yet progress is made, and the homes, scenery and flowers are beautiful along the spiraling way. Where did we obtain this modern day mania for constantly rushing everywhere while missing the joy of the journey?

To our modern society, instant often seems best; but nature refuses to adapt to this human rush-hour mentality. The green grass will return, the days will warm, and seeds will sprout and grow — but only in their traditionally allotted times and seasons. It still takes nine months for a baby to be born and more than twice that number, in years, for the child to grow to maturity. The face of the earth has changed but the human heart and the universal pulse of life still beat with their ancient unhurried pace. In our minds, we continue to travel winding, primitive paths. Discouragement slows our progress and depression can bring us to a halt. Each person's life is a unique pilgrim-journey where no one has yet cut through the mountains on our behalf, nor bridged the rivers. We, personally, must climb the hills and trudge the valleys which separate us from our goals. That is our challenge.

Recently a man was telling some of his friends about his oldest daughter who plays on the high school basketball team. He said, "She's like a tea bag; you never know how strong she is until she's in hot water." Those are the circumstances which bring forth the best from within. If it were not for the "hot water" times, we might never realize the real powers we possess. As each of us travels the primitive road of self-fulfillment, we cut our own paths and determine the pace. It's always slow. Anxiously, we want to move with the speed of life in the fast lane. When we are unable, we become frustrated. Within, it's tough going — step by step. We need to be reminded that we are here not simply to rush from place to place but to meet the people and learn some wisdom along the way.

Some people are made to feel small and

useless, like a tiny island time forgot, but each one is significant and should not be bypassed or ignored. Together, we form the community of earth. The poet John Donne wrote, "we are part of the mainland," with our own contribution to make. Life is a journey, but a journey of the heart as well as the feet. If we think life is only to get from point "A" to point "B," then we've missed the whole point of life.

In his popular book, *The Road Less Traveled*, Scott Peck begins his opening chapter with a sentence of only three words. Peck says if you can understand the meaning of these three words you need not read the book. The three words are: "Life is difficult." He proceeds to explain that if we totally accept this profound truth, then life will cease to be difficult.

I remember one of the little "charmers" by Hallmark in the newspaper several years ago. A small boy was beside his bicycle holding a tire pump and viewing his flat front tire. His Scottish Terrier was nearby, offering encouragement. The caption read: "Problems are challenges in disguise." These are the events which all must face. Either we lift up our hands in disgust or accept our problems as another challenge. Problems restrict our progress and tax our energies. Challenges, however, affect us differently. They energize us. If we could dismiss our problems by renaming them "challenges," perhaps the change of name would help us change our attitude. Solutions then may come more readily.

Patience and long-suffering are required of

all. Some have paid dearly. There is the sad case of Samuel A. Mudd (1833-1883). He was the doctor who set John Wilkes Booth's broken leg after he had assassinated President Lincoln. The public labeled him a conspirator, although he claimed he did not recognize Booth as Lincoln's assassin. He said that, as a doctor, he was required to help any injured person. However, Mudd was tried by a military court and found guilty as an accessory after the fact. He was sentenced to life in prison. Still this doctor did not lose faith in himself. He simply continued to do what he did best and saved the lives of prisoners and guards during the severe yellow-fever epidemic. Just as he had not neglected Booth, he did not neglect his guards and fellow prisoners. Mudd could easily have turned bitter over his unfortunate fate and refused to serve. Instead, he used his time and abilities in his new "circumstances." Four years later he was vindicated and freed.

Fatigue and discouragement can make cowards of us all as we search for reasons to continue our efforts. One day we may feel as helpless as a declawed alley cat but the following sunrise seems to bring a new purpose. Current studies continue to support the theory that depression and exhaustion are medically linked in the now prevalent disease known as Chronic Fatigue Syndrome. Before you dial the psychiatrist, get a good night's sleep. You may be more normal than you want to believe. Although life is difficult there is hope and help. The remedies to these basic problems may be rather simple and natural.

Problems are a part of every day's agenda and since they can't be avoided, we need to have a philosophy of coping. I once heard a minister say that, as a young man, he used to solve his problems. Now that he is older, he copes with them.

I can't begin to tell you the many times I've been thoroughly discouraged. I've often felt like pulling over to the side of the road and lifting my hood. In reality, all I needed was a word of encouragement, a restful day off, or an appreciative thanks. Then I was all right and back on the road again.

It is also helpful to adopt a positive attitude about pain. Realize pain is not our enemy but a vigilant friend. It tells us when the environment is hostile. Without this early warning system, our lives would be in constant jeopardy.

One day a man walked into a dentist's office and requested to have a tooth filled. The dentist was about to give him a shot of Novocaine when the man said he didn't want it. "I don't feel pain," he said. Then he explained there were only two times in his life when he felt pain. "One time," he said, "I was bear hunting and wanted to rest for a few minutes by a tree, and sat right in a big bear trap." The dentist sympathized, "Oh my, with those large steel teeth clamped into your behind, I'll bet you were in agony." The man nodded, "Yes sir, I was on my feet in an instant."

"Well, when was the second time you felt pain?" the dentist asked. The man replied: "When I ran out of chain." Hopefully, our painful experiences will not be so dramatic.

How often we don't attempt something worth while because we fear the pain of effort and possible failure. Instead of getting into the action we prefer to stay on the sideline sitting on the bench. Perhaps we tell ourselves that we are observing and learning from that position. The only thing we learn sitting on the bench is how to drink water. Life is too short to remain there. We must be a part of the action. Pain and inconvenience are the price of any genuine success.

If we continually postpone what we need to do, waiting for the ideal conditions, the end of life will find us waiting still. Excuses may make us feel better but they don't pay the rent. Utopia, you know, is only imaginary. There is an old axiom: "We can not always wait for our ship to come in; sometimes we must swim out to meet it."

A college professor once told his students before an examination that he didn't want to hear their complaints about grades. "Don't tell me," he said, "what you could have done in better circumstances." He explained maybe their grades would have been higher if they had had more time to study; if the exam had been held in the afternoon, or if the room had been quieter or cooler. He said they must learn to prove themselves in whatever situation they are. "You'll never have ideal conditions," he said. "People are judged, not on what they could have done in better circumstances, but on what they actually did accomplish in the conditions they encountered at the time."

After all, it's not the accomplishment of easy

goals that makes us happy but the realization of more difficult ones. The more effort required, the more outstanding the achievement. The interstate mentality must be laid aside when it comes to reaching the mountain peaks. The road which leads to the top is gradual and usually difficult. Yet the misty peaks continue to attract us for vacation, adventure and contemplation. Their pinnacles invite us to the heights where we can be uplifted in ecstasy. We come to explore their rock-ribbed walls and to find the treasures of buried time. We regard the mountains as sacred places as did the ancients who believed the gods lived in the heights.

Those who live according to the interstate mentality calculate how many miles they can cover in a certain amount of time. Thus, for them, mountains hold no mystique; instead they are barriers to be avoided. Yet they cannot be avoided or ignored for they cover one fifth of the surface of the earth. Perhaps they are nature's way to slow us down to compel us to view the beauty about us and provoke us to dream beyond the mundane present. Thus, our "mountains" are blessings in disguise which enable us to develop in body, mind and spirit.

There is a colloquial term called "shun-piking." It means avoiding the interstates and taking the back roads where we come into contact with the real world and better understand true values.

Each day we are on some primitive, dirt-covered back road in our minds. Those are the types made famous by a popular CBS commentator. In the Foreword to his book *On the Road with Charles Kuralt*, he says: "I have tried to go slow, stick to the back roads, take time to meet people, listen to yarns, notice the countryside go by, and feel the seasons change." It's on the back roads where Kuralt has found so much true success and continual hope for our country. The interstate means speed and easy traveling. That's the fast lane. Personal progress, character development, true learning and meaningful human encounters must all take a different route and a slower pace.

3

WE CAN'T GO ALONE

If you open an encyclopedia to the name of Albrecht Durer, you will be told he was a German painter and engraver during the Renaissance. His 58 years were lived between 1471-1528 and he was one of Germany's most creative artists. Some of his works will be listed and information given about his influence on Europe and the world. The encyclopedia will not tell you about Franz Knigstein, his friend, to whom he owed his success. I'll tell you.

Albrecht and Franz, as young men, were struggling to become artists. Both had raw talent but few funds. They devised a plan to assist each other achieve their goals. One would work to support the other until his university education was completed: then the other would sell his paintings to finance his friend's education. They drew lots to decide which one would attend school first. Durer was the winner. He went to art school and Knigstein took a job of hard manual labor to support him.

After years of study and artistic productions, Durer was selling his paintings and he returned to keep his part of the bargain. Only then did he realize the tremendous price his friend had paid. Knigstein's delicate and sensitive fingers had been ruined by years of rugged manual labor. Although he had to abandon his artistic dream, he rejoiced in his friend's success.

One day when Knigstein was kneeling with his rugged, gnarled hands intertwined in prayer, Durer quickly sketched the hands of his friend and completed what we now call the "Praying Hands." Today, art galleries the world over feature the works of Albrecht Durer, but the people's favorite is the "Praying Hands" inspired by his friend.

This story of the "Praying Hands" was shared with me many years ago by a dear friend. The author is anonymous. I have reread it many times. When I begin to lament the selfishness of some people, this story helps me keep a more balanced view.

I imagine that during his life Albrecht Durer must have thought a million times of how his success had actually been achieved by the hands of his friend, Franz Knigstein.

Similar stories are to be found in the lives of each of us. There is absolutely nothing we have done or can do which does not depend on the assistance of other people. Success is never the sum total of one person's efforts. We do not function alone. We can't.

Several years ago I read a newspaper article about a very successful business man. At that time he was in his mid-fifties and a millionaire. Today he continues to hold several important positions and obviously associates with influential people. As a young person, he had endured many hardships and personal tragedies and his family lived in poverty. The article told of them coming from Western Europe to the United States and quoted him as saying, "I worked for everything I got and nobody gave me anything."

I found that statement very arrogant and untruthful. Granted, he had difficulties and did work hard. But such a statement, "Nobody gave me anything," tells me he's very narrow-minded. I wanted to shout, "Were you not granted citizenship in a land of freedom and opportunity? Were your rights not secured by laws which were enforced by the courts? Were you not personally safeguarded by police and your property afforded fire protection? Did not someone offer you a job by which you began amassing your millions? Others built the roads you traveled, established the factories where you worked and had set a government in operation. Free enterprise was functioning and untold other gifts were freely handed to you."

Does this man, I wondered, not understand or appreciate the incredible number of people who died to achieve these priceless benefits? How dare he say, "Nobody gave me anything"!

Name something you have not received. The advantages which have come, and continue to come to us from others, are countless. It is not only a sign of ingratitude; it's blatant stupidity to think of ourselves or anyone as a self-made person.

Great minds have a deeper and more appreciative understanding of the priceless contributions of others. I've long been impressed by the words of Albert Einstein. "A hundred times every day," he said, "I remind myself that my inner and outer life depend on the labors of others, living and dead; and that I must exert myself in order to give in the same measure as I have received and am still receiving." Now there's a smart man. I can't fully appreciate the deep meaning of $E=MC^2$, but I can appreciate and applaud Einstein's wisdom when he attributes his success to the labors of others. This scientific genius clearly understood he was not a self-made man.

The observation is often made today that we are a narcissistic society. We grasp for everything we can selfishly obtain. There is little thought of bearing the burdens of others who are less fortunate. If we are rich or comfortably secure, do we ever think that another's poverty may have been the price of our prosperity?

A small number of people have hoarded land and minerals and become very wealthy. They acquired these possessions, justly or otherwise, but they did not create them. They only obtained and used them. This control and use of possessions by a few has left the majority poor. Even so, the old affluent names like Rockefeller, Ford, Carnegie, Dupont, etc., have assisted others through employment opportunities plus grants and foundations for society. Today, this sense of responsibility to others is nearly lost, for the "nouveau riche" often turn more inward than outward.

Millionaires needed the help of others to amass their fortunes. Now, others need help to sustain their lives. That's why the wealthy have a moral obligation to society. All people, rich, poor and middle class, are part of one human community, called to live in unity with each other. The old maxim is: "United we stand, divided we fall."

Years ago our country decided it could no longer live in isolation from the rest of the world. We then started thinking as a part of the global community. All realistic people subscribe to that philosophy. This becomes truer each day as our means of travel and communication put us directly in touch with the lives of people everywhere on earth. Please be convinced that we, as individuals, can't live isolated lives, anymore than our country can.

When I say we can not survive without the assistance of others, I'm reminded of a small tree I once saw in Wyoming. It was growing out of a rock, and a plaque explained its inspiring story. "The original line of the Union Pacific Railroad passed within a few feet of this point, and supposedly was deflected slightly to avoid destruction of this tree. The firemen of each passing train never failed to drench the tree with a bucket of water." Some call it a natural phenomenon but perhaps it should be seen as a cooperative human endeavor.

There are times in the lives of all when we are struggling to survive, similar to that tree. Many of us would have wilted and died had it not been for those buckets of kindness, help, and love bestowed upon us. To "bloom where you are planted," is not always an easy task. The roots of some people have been well-nourished, while others have been deprived. Even the rich, strong and healthy stand in need of others, more than many of them would like to admit. The golden rule still applies: do for others what we would like done for us. Such a rule is not always easy but it is always right.

The rich didn't obtain their money without the assistance of many people and they most certainly can't continue their life-style without the help of others. No one is a self-made or self-sustaining individual, especially those who live above the norm. They, like the rest of us, could not survive without the thousands of services of society. If the wealthy are dependent on others, we can be certain that the poor are even more dependent. Everybody needs somebody.

When called upon to donate money or time to some cause in the school, church or community we often inquire, what's in it for me? That's the wrong question to ask. It implies our debts to the past have all been paid and we owe nothing to society or to anyone in it. The fact is we have many unpaid debts from the past. Our contributions today are simply little bits of restitution. When we look to the future we often become fearful and cling to our security. Looking back, however, in a spirit of gratitude, makes us appreciate what society has done for us. It's the backward glance which should motivate us to give support as we have been supported. Our gifts and donations are not magnanimous offerings from our hearts' generosity, but unpaid debts for past favors. Others have paid our way, now we need to return the favor. Shame on us for our sad record of selfishness, in leaving the scandalous national debt and a polluted world to our grandchildren.

Years ago I read a story, written in verse, telling the dismal results which occurred because people wouldn't assist each other. Six men were without shelter on a sub-zero night. They were gathered in a circle around a warm, burning fire. Each sat on his own individual log. When the fire began to burn low, no one would donate his log. Each person had some prejudiced excuse. One, sitting in the circle, was very poor. He would not give his log to warm a rich man. The rich man judged the poor man as lazy and refused to give his log for him. Another would not donate to warm an African-American in the circle. In turn, this man remembered past racial hurts and tightly clung to his log. The final two members didn't contribute to the fire because they belonged to different religions. The final stanza read: "The logs held tight in icy hands, were proof of human sin; they didn't die from the cold without, they died from the cold within."

The whole idea of the Social Security System is based on the principle that people need people. We have discovered the best way to find individual security is through social security. The Social Security System has been called "a contract between the ages." It's based on the theory that people will help each other.

Someone explained the difference of how a Conservative and Liberal assist others. If there's a drowning man 50 feet out in a lake calling for help, a Conservative will throw him a 25-foot rope. The man must prove he's deserving of help by swimming the first 25 feet on his own. The Liberal, however, will throw out a 50-foot rope. When the drowning man grabs it, the Liberal will let go of his end to hurry off to do some more good deeds.

Eleanor Roosevelt shines as an example of a genuinely caring, humanitarian-centered person of our society. Her wealth and high position caused her to reach out to the unfortunate multitudes. She worked with the young and fought for equal rights for minority groups. The powerful and wealthy today need the spirit of that distinguished public figure and very active First Lady in our American history. If many of her attitudes and ideals were lived, we would have a much better world.

As a young boy growing up on the farm, I was always impressed by the threshing days. Neighbors had to assist each other with tractors, wagons and workers. All the jobs were being done simultaneously. It created a mutual respect, made people dependent on others, and built a strong community. Then came the combine.

Technology surged ahead and sociability pulled back.

In the area where I now live, there are many Amish families. They understand that no one succeeds all by themselves. One person can not raise a barn in a day, but the community can. They don't invest in expensive insurance policies for they, personally, are each other's "insurance."

Know this as a fact, we can't go through life alone — even if we wanted to. Nor can we deny that others gave us precious gifts in the past which we enjoy today. Never be so brash to say, "Nobody ever gave me anything." Our assets are held only temporarily, so while we have some control over them, why not share with others? It's often said, the only things we ever keep are those we give away.

4

MAKING THE MOST
OF WHAT YOU HAVE

Flora Wellman — *born* in Massillon, Ohio — moved to San Francisco at an early age. Her poverty-filled young life was further complicated in 1876 by the birth of a baby boy, born out of wedlock. Later, she married a farmer by the name of London. Her son received very little formal education. He was on the streets selling papers at age ten and working in the local cannery at fourteen. When he turned eighteen, he became a hobo.

The need for money and the desire to improve his life soon persuaded him to begin his own program of self education; sometimes reading and writing twenty hours a day. He especially concentrated on the works of Darwin, along with Marx and Nietzsche.

At age twenty-one, the lure of Alaskan gold enticed him to the Klondike. Six years later he wrote *The Call of the Wild*. It boosted him into celebrity status and, at age 29, Jack London was the highest paid and most widely read writer in America.

One can hardly imagine such outstanding literary accomplishments by a poverty-stricken, erratic young man. But in retrospect, if Jack London had had a better formal education, or a more secure home life, he would have been deprived of those rich experiences which energized his life and writing. In all, he wrote over 50 books in which he championed the philosophy of "the survival of the fittest."

I still remember the thrill of reading *The Call of the Wild* in the fifth grade. I had to brush away a few tears when Buck was stolen from his peaceful California home and harnessed to a sled on the frigid Klondike trail. I rejoiced as he grew stronger and cheered when he finally subdued Spitz, his savage nemesis, to become the leader of the team. I could understand his breaking away and leading a wild wolf pack when his kind master, John Thornton, was killed. And who could fail to be moved when Buck returned each year to visit the site of John Thornton's death?

In my grade-school reading of the novel, I thought of it as only a dog story. I knew little about the author and less of philosophies, evolutionary theories, and the applications of this story to the human level. Now I understand that Jack London was painting a vivid picture of the ideas he had found in Darwin. No doubt those same teachings had inspired him to succeed, for he could have easily blamed the fate of his early life and done nothing.

Someone described London as dedicated to creating people who were red-blooded heroes.

He wanted to show "men with the bark on." His prolific pen would make one think he was a self-confident, accomplished man, whose ideas spontaneously flowed into his many books — as abundantly as water filling buckets. Most likely, the opposite picture would be more accurate. He must have felt inferior and unsure of himself, secretly envying those who had enjoyed a more stable childhood. He was unaware of the identity of his father. Although his early life experiences gave him material for his books, he no doubt wondered what more he could have accomplished with a more formal education. It appears he was writing to give himself courage — to be as strong as his heroes.

Buck, the heroic champion in *The Call of the Wild*, is more like a person than a dog. We know only as many of his canine feelings and thoughts as the writer reveals to us. The author speaks of Buck, but actually he is relating his own fears, hurts and hopes. Jack London gives a lingering glimpse into his uncertain origin by making Buck, not a pedigreed dog, but half St. Bernard and half Scottish sheep dog. Buck goes from California to Alaska, a symbol of two extremes: from South to North; from leisure to work; from warmth to bitter cold; and from a shiftless existence to fulfilling a lofty challenge. He not only survives but triumphs as the author illustrates the Darwinian theme that survival is possible, if one can make the proper adaptation to existing circumstances.

The concept is an exciting one, stirring the very soul and giving confidence and energy to the timid. It's little wonder this classic story of the sled dog has gone through dozens of printings and was translated into sixty-eight languages.

The world is full of people today who are facing these same ancient struggles. They've been neglected or abused as children. They've been raised in the slums and have barely been able to survive. Their formal education has been inadequate or non existing. Perhaps a life of crime is the only "work" for which they have been prepared. These people are ready to walk the wild side of life and they know their future may well be a small iron-barred prison cell. The teaching in this story says these people can make an about-face. They can go to the opposite extreme and be productive and successful.

The life and works of Jack London can challenge anyone at any age. It says not to feel inferior because of weak beginnings, poor education or a shiftless past. You may be living a very difficult life, but realize there are productive strengths and abilities within you which have been lying dormant. Why not put them to the test? Obviously, there are some who are unable to function on their own because of physical, mental or emotional deficiencies. They need continual assistance and direction from others. Those we must care for. But here I speak to average capable people who can't find the motivation to begin or to continue and who feel nearly defeated by discouragement.

If you can classify yourself as an ordinary individual, then understand that you have the strength within to meet your challenges. Know your unique qualities and appreciate your own precious set of genes and circumstances. Review your family background and note the desirable traits among your ancestors. You have undoubtedly inherited some of these. Think of your personal experiences. How have these enlightened and prepared you for some future endeavor? Realize no one else can achieve those objectives quite like you, for no one else has your exact sentiments, inherited your characteristics nor lived your personal experiences. If these have been positive, then you know what to imitate. If negative, then you know what to avoid. Interview yourself and be sure you know who you are.

Any of us could find a lengthy list of personal deficiencies, but why concentrate on them? We don't need to constantly remind ourselves of what a lady frequently told her husband: "When it comes to self improvement, no one has more potential." Too often, we regret what we don't have and overlook our true treasures. We need to think big and be glad we can think, see, laugh, enjoy food, shelter and friends. These make us richer than a millionaire in the things which really matter. For these qualities we need to be continually thankful and, from such a solid basis, go on to outstanding achievements.

This philosophical outlook of appreciating how enriched we are today, could vastly improve the whole spectrum of society. Take this example. A jewelry store display-case is left unlocked. No store personnel are nearby. A customer could "lift" a dozen diamond rings and quietly leave. About to steal the rings, the would-be thief reconsiders. I possess the gift of life; I have opportunities, peace of mind, and I cherish my freedom. Are not these intangible values worth more than a dozen little pieces of hard stone and metal? Maybe the diamond rings would be worth $25,000. I run a big risk of being arrested. Even if I didn't get caught, what do I need to buy for $25,000? Can I use it to purchase a better life, increased opportunity, peace of mind or more freedom? I'm already rich in these areas. Wouldn't the stolen rings cause me to lose, rather than gain, something? I'd be running scared, feeling threatened and guilty. It's absolutely not worth it. It's a terrible transaction to make. If I steal the rings I will have thrown away values worth many millions of dollars to obtain something worth a mere fraction. I'll be running scared, under the fear of severe punishment. Is that what we call being smart? That's why, I've said and repeat again, we must truly value what we already have. To throw away precious values for ones of far lesser worth is to demonstrate the height of ignorance.

We have an insatiable desire to grab too much, and appear to be something we are not. T.S. Eliot informed his generation that most of the trouble in the world is caused by people wanting to be important. Religion, ethics, citizenship and common sense forbid us to buy our pleasures at such a high price. Imagine what genuine gifts we could be to those lacking in self-esteem, if we would enrich them with meaningful praise and encouragement. Collectively, we already possess the means necessary to appreciably change the world for the better.

Should we not put ourselves through a type of basic training, simply to emphasize and re-appreciate our natural gifts and abilities? When people enter the military, they are required to undergo basic training. During that time recruits learn to be deprived of certain comforts. This may be the first time in their lives they've been pushed beyond their will and deprived of what they desire. It may be running two miles, doing a hundred pushups, or adhering to a particular diet. Only then, do they begin to realize how easy life had been. The little inconveniences they used to complain about are quickly forgotten. This experience forces the participants to rethink their values and view their situations from a different, more positive perspective.

Taking what we have, whether it be great or small, and using it to the very best of our abilities, propels us toward our desired goals. Thus we become a little bit of all we experience. One person said, "When I was a small boy I wanted to grow up and become the President of the United States. My dream never came true. Well," he added, "it become half true. I did grow up." A person's character is relatively easy to understand. It is simply one's habits which are long continued. If we want to change our character, we adopt a different set of habits for a long period of time. That's part of growing up.

Some coaches tell their players, "When we

win we build confidence, when we lose we build character." One year a team finishes last, having such a poor record they could qualify for Federal Aid. The very next season, the same players come back to be the best. What has happened? In the meantime, they looked within themselves and some better attitudes and habits were established. They came to the realization that before you can finish first, you must first finish. The basics enable us to finish. Improving the basics enables us to finish first.

Answer for yourself what you want to do in this world. "Is there a life before death?" What does it mean to me? How do I intend to live it? This world is not only for the experts and the super-talented. It's for all. There is a place and in fact a definite need for you and me to be here. Without us, the scene would be incomplete. I often recall the words of John Audubon: "The world would be very silent," he said, "if no birds sang, except those that sang best."

5

DON'T EVEN TRY
TO PLEASE EVERYONE

Many years ago I visited Fort Sumter, S.C., the site of the first battle of the Civil War. I still vividly remember the young red-haired tour guide who told a tragic story of how the war had devastated one family.

He said two brothers from Kentucky left home the same day to enlist in the military. The older joined the Confederacy and the younger offered his allegiance to the Union. In the midst of one intense battle, the older brother was killed in action. The Confederate government shipped his body home to Kentucky, where his grieving father buried him in a small plot on the family farm.

Several months later the younger brother was also killed in action. His body, still dressed in the blue uniform of the North, was likewise returned home to Kentucky.

The twice-grieved father now faced the awkward dilemma as to where he should bury his younger son. Since both brothers had fought and died for opposing causes, he thought it might be improper to bury them side by side. But the more he considered the matter, the more he became convinced the brothers should lie beside each other. Thus, he buried the younger son beside his brother. One stone marked their graves, on which was inscribed: "Here are buried two brothers. Each fought and died for a cause he thought was right. Divided in life; united in death."

Many of our choices must be made where there is no precedent to follow. Sometimes we, too, may choose to disregard an established criterion. In those situations we depend on logical reasons and good judgment. Our decisions may disappoint some people but that can't be helped. It's simply a by-product of decision-making and there is no way to avoid it.

The two brothers did not feel constrained to join the same cause, either to please their father or each other. The father, likewise, felt perfectly free to make his choice in regard to their burial. We don't know if the two brothers would have chosen to be buried beside each other. Most likely they never discussed their burial site, for they planned to return home alive. Since death was their fate, their sorrowful father had to select their graves according to his judgment. No doubt many disagreed with his decision in such a sensitive matter, while others agreed. Isn't that the way with most decisions? Had you been in the father's position, what choice would you have made?

I once read the results of a survey which said, "Even if decisions are unpopular, the majority of people stand in admiration of those who clearly state their views and act accordingly." When we try to please everyone we please no one, including ourselves.

People have often asked me what they should do in certain circumstances. I think it's impossible in most cases to give others detailed information on how to act. We all wonder at times what's the right thing to do. As the movie says, "Do The Right Thing." For numerous questions there is no established precedent to follow. Each person ultimately bears the burden of his or her own decisions. What we've read, heard, been told and reasoned out, all go into our decisions. In the case of the two brothers, I wonder if their father was influenced by the Kentucky State motto: "United We Stand, Divided We Fall." The young men were divided and fell but their memories remain united. Thus the family still stands together.

The psychologist Dr. Murray Banks likes to present his wisdom in a humorous manner, taken from his Jewish background. He gives a list of guidelines under the title of: "A Recipe for Sanity." One ingredient in the recipe is to avoid making your decisions solely on the premise of trying to please others. He also says people admire those who have strong convictions, even if they don't agree with them. We are to seek the answer which seems to us as most correct and fair. We have our personal convictions and realize others have theirs. Sensitivity and understanding are therefore required in all human relations and decisions, for our decisions affect others.

A great number of churches today subscribe to the modern concept of ecumenism. It means people of various denominations can worship, work and socialize, in a spirit of unity. Ecumenism calls people to be resolute in their personal convictions, but at the same time, respect others' beliefs. Members of one church or denomination are not to be pressured to join another. The key word is pressured. In our world we can live with a wonderful sense of unity without insisting on uniformity. People are to believe and practice as they see fit and we are to show a sacred respect for the values of others. Such conduct makes for peacefulness and encourages people who think differently to still be friends. That's the way it's supposed to be.

Organizations, as well as families, are often divided by those who have too many answers and try to force others to accept "the truth." They are welcomed into the group about as much as a case of measles. The human mind and heart are delicate and should not be threatened or forced into anything. To demand others to think a certain way or pressure them against their will, is a clear case of conscience abuse.

Certain people become controversial simply because of the jobs they hold. This is the case with politicians, judges, juries, police, and in fact anyone who must make decisions which affect others. Teenagers frequently remind parents of their "ridiculous rules." A vivid example of a job which invites division and criticism is that of the umpire. This person always works in the midst of a sharply divided crowd. When a questionable decision makes one side happy, it automatically makes the other side angry.

Imagine the chaotic situation which would result if an umpire in the World Series were to try to please everyone. Maybe he would feel very democratic and consult the fans about a particularly close call. How many of you think the runner was out? Let's see your hands. Now, all those who think he was safe! That umpire would have worked his last game. We, like the umpire, must follow the rule: "Call 'em and walk away." We will leave some cheering in approval and others screaming in protest. There is absolutely no way to please everyone and we all know it.

Wherever that inner drummer leads, the human heart must follow. Some feel obliged to conform to another and experience a sense of guilt if they try to make their own path through this world. These individuals need encouragement to be themselves, to make their own decisions and not feel obligated to walk the road laid out by another. If we fail to hear and follow the beat of our own heart, we are relinquishing our precious individuality.

This does not mean the drummer will always lead us down the road of boundless happiness to a carefree existence. The destination may be exactly the opposite. There are times when we, like those brave Chinese citizens, must face our

Tiananmen Squares. But why put our lives on the line? To be true to ourselves and to our own convictions. We are simply acknowledging the sound of our inner drummer and, if honest, we must march to its unique beat.

None of us enjoys being opposed or contradicted by others so we seldom express our true feelings. Some of us try to avoid controversy at all costs. We would rather open the door to Dante's Inferno than engage in a confrontation with another. Keeping quiet and keeping peace, may sound like the heroic thing to do, but that action often results in a confrontation with ourselves.

An evangelist was preaching on TV, trying to "save" everyone in the audience. He asked one man, whom he had invited to the stage, if he had "gotten the Holy Spirit." The gentleman replied, "I don't want to get the Spirit. I want the Spirit to get me." We want the truth to get us. Truth is one, but we are many. When we are all making a concerted effort to follow the truth, we may be acting differently but correctly. When the truth gets us, we will try to please the truth rather than others.

Most of the trouble in this world is caused when people start comparing themselves to others. When someone was asked about the work he did, he replied, "I'm self-employed. I mind my own business." That same idea is voiced by the famous psychiatrist, Carl Rogers: "When we speak most individually," he said, "then we speak most universally." Minding our own business is not a narrow view but a very broad one. If everyone would mind their own business and do it well, we would have just reopened the door to an earthly paradise.

We can be so preoccupied with foolish non-essentials that we neglect our very basic truths and values. Some years ago 2300 federal employees in 12 Washington agencies were asked to sign their names to a particular document, if they accepted its teachings. Sixty-eight percent refused to sign. When asked where they thought the statement was from, some said, "The Christian Science Monitor," others "The National Catholic Observer," and still others "The Communist Manifesto." In reality it was a quotation from the Declaration of Independence. Can people understand and appreciate the workings of the federal government if they lack an elementary understanding of the basis of government?

There is a particular joy and sense of accomplishment in minding my own business. It may lead me to be alone but that does not mean I experience loneliness but rather a liberating solitude. Loneliness is a negative, a certain depressed state of being. It is something one would like to avoid. Solitude is a very positive term. It implies happiness and excitement in a project. True solitude is a very rich blessing.

Sometime ago I attended a workshop which was meant to help us know ourselves better, find inner peace, and live harmoniously with others. Three different mindsets were discussed and we were to judge which most applied to us. The presenter explained some people are aggressive and others are submissive. These two types don't please each other, nor do they share meaningful communications. In between these two extremes are the assertive people. The assertive have some aggressive feelings but use them in a limited way — just enough to make a clear point without dominating others. The assertive, likewise, have some submissive qualities but they refuse to be intimidated. They are neither the bulldozers nor the floor-mats. When we act in an assertive manner, we run the best chance of being accepted by others and approved by ourselves.

People will forgive others for many hurts, but most people find it very difficult to forgive those who have humiliated them. Perhaps we fear humiliating another if we state our views, or voice an objection. But if we have acted within the parameters of gentle assertiveness and another is offended, we still have acted correctly.

Human relationships remain a complicated and often touchy situation, but the one who tries to keep peace at all costs will soon discover the cost has been too high. It will especially take its toll on the submissive person who will pay in the form of ulcers, burnout, discouragement or even by becoming overly aggressive.

I once listened to an assertive man trying to convince a woman of the truthfulness of a story which was difficult to believe. He very aggressively tried to compel her to accept his unusual tale. I, likewise, thought his presentation had more imagination than truth. After ten minutes of bantering she still did not accept his story and decided to conclude the conversation in an imaginative manner. "Look," she said, "I may have been born at night, but it wasn't last night." The point was made directly but without anger. He said no more, but had no grounds to be offended or feel humiliated — nor did she.

We often read about short cuts to success. People frequently share their secrets on how to improve knowledge, lose weight, gain strength or become an overnight celebrity. We don't see anything written advising us on how to lose money, get out of shape, or waste our time. We can do all of those things pretty well without advice. If someone, however, were to write a book on how to fail, the first sentence should be: "The sure key to failure is to try to please everyone."

6

LAUGH OFTEN

An old mountain man who had lived in the Ozarks for seventy-five years was taking his first airplane flight, bound for Los Angeles. His plane took off just after dark, and fifteen minutes into the flight the pilot announced they had lost an engine and would arrive thirty minutes behind schedule.

Shortly, the pilot announced they had lost a second engine and would be one hour and fifteen minutes late. The people began to panic. Pandemonium only really erupted, though, when the pilot informed the wary passengers they had lost a third engine. The cockpit voice said they would arrive two hours and forty minutes behind schedule. Amidst the screams and cries, the old mountain man could be heard saying: "You know, if we lose another engine we're going to be up here all night."

There are all kinds of panic situations, which we constantly face or envision others facing. The reason we joke about them is that the joke makes light of the circumstances and sends our thinking off in another direction. It's an escape, often, from some unpleasant aspect of reality. Nobody imagines that the prospect of a plane crash could ever be funny but, in such a terrifying situation, someone's seemingly fearless comment gives us the courage to hope that somehow the plane won't crash after all. Humor thrives by leading us in one direction and suddenly presenting us with a completely unexpected conclusion.

We live with many fears and hurts. And, ironically, these are the stuff from which we normally construct our jokes. For that reason, it is said that the best humor originates in difficult times, rather than in those which are more pleasant. In happy times there's plenty of joy already present. It's when we lose hope and peace that we must manufacture both. Humor may be more responsible for survival than we think.

No one likes to age, face medical and legal problems, or be frightened about death. We are constantly puzzled by the mysterious ways the sexes relate to each other. These subjects supply much of the standard material for humor. We don't always have the answer to these complex and confusing aspects of our personal life, and so we create our own imaginative solutions which are often very comical. When we can laugh at ourselves and with others, it shows we are accepting our circumstances and trying to endure. It is certainly a healthier solution than crying or becoming depressed. Humor gives us something of a handle on the problem, at least momentarily and to some degree.

When we cause others to laugh, we exercise

a unique type of ministry: to console the afflicted and help the hurting. If we were Sigmund Freud we could analyze another's problems from a deep psychological perspective. To St. Peter, a spiritual explanation might be in order. A Shakespeare could write a beautiful sonnet to soothe the person's pain. Since we do not possess these super talents, we minister the best we can. For a person in deep sorrow, we try to be present in another way — with humor — to lighten the burden oppressing their heart. If we can help a troubled individual to smile or utter a little laugh, we are enabling that person to take a first step toward recovery.

Humor enables us to express ourselves and make a point on some subjects we could never explain in a profound way. How do you, for example, seriously tell others they are crude in their manners and irritating you? We may be unable or most uncomfortable to address the topic in a productive manner. But we can, at times, find a way to do so in a humorous way. If humor can achieve the desired results and leave a relationship intact, why not use it?

Once, shortly after I had moved to a certain parish, an elderly parishioner began to complain periodically about my style of ministry. He was very serious, quite sensitive and usually irritating. These minor concerns were life and death issues to him. I listened dispassionately with a cheerless face, trying to be professional. One day, when he came, I smiled, shook his hand and said, "Well, what are you going to gripe about today?"

It caught him off guard and broke the tension. For the first time he laughed and his attitude became friendly. We had our best talk and last complaint-centered visit. From then on things were better. My relaxed, humorous attitude accomplished what a serious, reasoned response never could have.

In the case of public speaking, a bit of levity serves as a barometer to determine if the audience is following your thoughts or merely daydreaming. The speaker might state the most profound truth since the invention of the wheel, and still elicit no reaction from the crowd. Did the people understand? Do they care? The speaker may not have a clue. Listeners may often appear to be deeply lost in thought, but are these inspired by what is being said or are they at the golf course, on a date, or reviewing tomorrow's office schedule? Even assuming they are listening, one often doesn't know if they agree. A bit of genuine humor, introduced at this point, could answer many of these questions. If the audience smiles or laughs, you know they are listening. The technique also serves as a pleasant change of pace and revives those who may be getting tired.

Laughter has been called the "sunshine of the soul." It produces warmth, light-heartedness, friendliness and is a pleasant means of sharing with others. Humor and consequent laughter melts away many icy tensions and frustrations which otherwise could grind us to a mental and emotional halt. It has been said that when we have a serious problem, the second best thing to do, next to finding a solution, is to find humor in it. That enables us to be accepting or, at least, more patient until a real solution is discovered.

The story has been repeated thousands of times, but the case of Norman Cousins remains the classic example of the valuable healing effects of humor. His cure, attributed to laughter, took place even though he was suffering the advanced stages of a connective tissues disease. His chances for recovery had been diagnosed as poor. Cousins took on a steady diet of old Marx Brothers movies and some of the Candid Camera shows and laughed his way to enduring good health.

This former editor of the "Saturday Review" went on to write his best-selling book, *Anatomy of An Illness*, and other works on achieving and maintaining good health. He became a self-directed authority on the inner workings of the healing process. Cousins demonstrated how we can often be cured by what he called the "doctor" who lives inside each of us.

That internal doctor is no joke. We begin the healing process by believing in the God-given curative powers of our own bodies and minds. If we encourage our minds and bodies to heal themselves, they will. The recovery will take place sooner, with better prognosis, in those who can relax, laugh, and think less of their sickness and more about the good health they wish to achieve. Humor is the catalysis which frees this inner doctor to work. Many of the medicines we need, according to Cousins, are contained in our own bodies. We carry within ourselves our own apothecary. This is not meant to downgrade traditional medicine which is obviously vital to our health. But medicine does not heal. It only assists. Ultimately, we must heal ourselves. Any assistance is more than welcome, but it is only that — assistance. If our minds and bodies are rebelling and uncooperative in the healing process, there is no medicine which will save us. "Dr. Humor" should be the first one called upon in a crisis situation. The first prescription should be a potion of laughter and levity to be taken at mealtime and before bed. Its purpose is to dispose the body for the healing process which is about to begin.

As previously stated, the best humor is produced not in carefree situations but in the midst of difficult times — war, flood, fire, heartbreak and illness. Obviously, laughter is not a cure-all. The Bible states: "Even in laughter the heart may be sad" (Proverbs 14:13). Yet the Bible assumes that laughter is a vital part of life and exists for the good of the person. Humor has a long and glorious history of driving sorrow from the human heart. People who are continually battling severe daily pains or difficulties need help. It may be the only pause that refreshes and sets their minds free to search for inner healing.

I once heard about a doctor who diagnosed a prisoner as having a serious disease. He gave him three years. The prisoner said he wasn't worried because the judge had given him ten. (Just a joke.)

Something we all do at least several times a day is eat. We naturally acquire a taste for good food. When it is of poor quality, it causes us some distress. We would expect food to be a popular subject on the humor list. I heard about the food at one restaurant which was so bad they printed the Heimlich Maneuver on the place mats. Choking is no "laughing matter," but if the food were that terrible and one was obliged to eat it, such a gesture might help one endure the situation. I met Dr. Heimlich at the Buckeye Book Fair in Wooster, Ohio in 1991 and told him that joke, which he said he had never heard. He thought it was quite funny.

Humor and laughter can be used to take the edge off an unpleasant experience which is already past, with no hope of changing. Take, for example, the football coach who had a miserable season. When asked how the year went he replied his team went five and five. "We lost five on the road, and five at home." It still adds up to a miserable record but the humor helped the coach and players to accept the results. Humor releases tension and gives a shift of emphasis, which makes it easier to endure an unpleasant reality. It's certainly better to joke and laugh about one's defeats and failures than to brood over them, become depressed and make everyone else miserable in the process.

Isn't it surprising how a complex problem is made to look simpler with the use of humor? Once there was a poor man who married a wealthy widow. They appeared to others as being very happy, but within a year their divorce papers were finalized. Neighbors and friends wanted to know what had gone wrong. Someone explained, "She wanted to be romanced; he wanted to be financed." That provided a closure to the problem and offered a caveat for others.

It has been said, "If you can laugh at a good joke, it's a sign of good mental health." The poet Ella Wheeler Wilcox is remembered for those famous lines of her poem entitled *Solitude*:

> "Laugh, and the world laughs with you;
>   Weep, and you weep alone;
> For the sad old earth
>   must borrow its mirth,
>   But has trouble enough of its own."

How much better life would be if the whole world would laugh more and fight less.

The title of this chapter advises us to "laugh often." That doesn't mean a silly, giggly laugh or one that is completely nonsensical. It doesn't mean laughing because you've had a few drinks, or because something vulgar has been said. Real healing humor is of a different kind. It's not a cop-out or an avoidance mechanism. Rather, it faces reality, and addresses the tough times in its own unique way. Humor helps us survive. It gives us something to do when we don't know what to do. It's the choice we make for a temporary solution until we can find a more permanent one. It's a response to true-life situations. Humor has a long impressive record of helping people to live life more fully, and it possesses a promising future. If you think there may be tough times ahead, then you'd better develop your sense of humor and get ready for tomorrow.

7

DIFFERENT PACES
FOR DIFFERENT RACES

It's not difficult to run a mile. Millions of people can do it. You simply set an easy pace and jog along until you complete the distance. If you want to run a fast or competitive mile, then that's a different story. In the whole world, there is but a small, select group of men who can run a mile under four minutes. Since Roger Bannister of Great Britain ran the first sub-four-minute mile (3.59.4) in 1954, only one United States runner has held the world's record. He is Jim Ryun. Ryun reigned as king of the milers for nine years: 1966-1975. His best time was 3.51.1.

In 1974, I attended a two-day training camp near Cleveland, Ohio, with a group of cross-country runners. The second day we spent with the reigning world record holder, Jim Ryun. He spoke to us, answered questions, showed slides of the past Olympics and then led us in one of his strenuous workouts. He expressed a number of views which impressed me very much. Here are a few of them.

Jim Ryun said that running is ninety percent mental attitude and ten percent physical strength. That I found truly amazing. He said you must set your mind to a regular workout schedule and make sure you keep it. You need to have a goal in mind, a time you truly believe you can achieve, and that becomes your dominant driving force. If you're not mentally convinced you can do it, you'll never do it.

He said nobody runs a hard mile without some pain; the faster the mile, the more the pain. You can't allow the pain to dominate you. Try to imagine you don't feel any pain. If that doesn't help, remind yourself the pain won't kill you. All the while, you must sustain and even increase that merciless pace, which separates the winners from the runners.

Ryun told us, when he was a high school freshman in Kansas he went out for track simply to be with his friends who were trying out. After a few sessions, the coach said he didn't have the ability to be a good runner and he was dropped from the team.

In his sophomore year he tried again and this time he made the team. Two years later, Jim Ryun astonished the entire sports world by becoming the second high school boy in history to break the four-minute mile. After that, sports writers began to spell his name correctly. Previously, many had been spelling it Ryan. He continued to pursue other running goals and achieved most of them.

All of us enjoyed that day spent with this

international celebrity. He even posed with us individually for a picture. Many commentators, coaches and spectators say the mile run is the highlight of the track meet. I agree. For me, the anticipation of the mile always took on an added excitement when I knew Jim Ryun would be in it.

Running an easy mile is like living an easy life — no pain, no sweat, no particular commitment to any cause. But the person who wants to achieve difficult goals and accomplish worthwhile objectives, must pay the demanding price of pain and sacrifice.

Every person has a life to live, a work to accomplish, a mile to run. Some take their obligations very lightly and run for fun. Others run for their lives. In his Letter to the Corinthians, St. Paul told the early Christians to "run so as to win" (1 Cor 9:24). Whether running, working, or simply living, it's good to remember that one's mental attitude makes all the difference.

Although the fast pace is thrilling and brings the crowd to its feet, it's not the only pace which leads to victory. In our lives, we compete in many arenas. Depending on the circumstances, sometimes the winner is the one who has less speed but tremendous perseverance. The day by day efforts and the consistent commitment to quality work, will also bring us to the victory circle. That, in fact, is the real test of stamina. The athlete endures the pain of oxygen deficit and straining muscles but it's only for a while. Perseverance is especially necessary for any long term commitments.

Who has not heard the famous tale of "The Tortoise and the Hare"? Now that's a change of pace. The hare is equipped with blazing speed as compared to the tortoise, but the hare becomes careless, even lazy. The hare thinks there is no challenge. The tortoise, however, with its plodding stride, knows it must set a determined and steady pace. Eventually the tortoise wins the race. The victory goes not to the fastest or the most skillful, but to the one who is most persistent. Again we note, speed is not always the key to victory.

Since the time of Aesop in 550 B.C., the story of his victorious tortoise has surely given courage to many of his fellow Greeks and people the world over. Aesop confirms the view that achievements do not always go to the most skillful or qualified people. He says the reward is reserved for those who believe they can be successful and who persevere until they are.

History is replete with stories of capable men and women who sought to achieve their goals but became sidetracked and frustrated along the way. In the wake of their initial failures, some could not recover. They did a few fast dashes but were simply unable to endure the long run. Others persevered harder after each setback and eventually realized their long-denied dreams.

Abraham Lincoln's life story demonstrates the epitome of perseverance. Many of his contemporaries would never have considered him the most accomplished man of his time. Today we believe that he is. Certainly he's the most remembered. His formal education was meager, delayed and very primitive. Perseverance kept pushing him to read, reread, think, write and advance in wisdom. His physical appearance was the subject of ridicule, and his gestures were called awkward. He did not appear to be a great statesman in the making. Lincoln's star rose very slowly. He met with one political defeat after another. Yet, there was within him some deep inner strength which refused to be conquered. It kept moving him toward his goal. Had he progressed at a faster pace, he would have peaked before his time. His many defeats were all part of his education and when his country called for him, he was there. Progress is normally slower than we like, but in the long run it may be right on schedule.

How many, in a frantic state of anxiety, try to achieve instant success? Even tomorrow is too long to wait, it must be today. Furthermore, they want to do it painlessly. This attitude reflects the narcissistic symptoms of our age. These are not the lessons history has taught us. "The pursuit of even the best things ought to be calm and tranquil." That advice was offered to the citizens of Rome nearly 2000 years ago by one of their wisest statesmen, Marcus Cicero. It is also timely counsel for our own times. These sudden bursts of speed toward riches and easy street, may cause some to lose the small amounts of money they already possess. The get-rich-fast enthusiasts often turn to the lottery or other quick-fix pursuits.

Too many live by the "mad dash mentality," instead of formulating a plan and deliberately and persistently moving toward its fulfillment. Once we identify the race, then we set the pace.

It is difficult to be content when we can't see ourselves making rapid progress. Yet the important question to ask is: are we moving in the right direction? If the direction is correct, then we will arrive, even though the pace seems slower than erosion. If we're on the right track and making progress, that's encouraging. It's the old tortoise story again, where persistence wins over speed.

For a number of years, I read a column in our daily newspaper by Sam Shulsky. He gave advice about investing and other uses of money. In one column he told an affluent widow she had saved enough and should begin spending some. Later, an elderly gentleman wrote an objection. He said, money should be saved, not spent. He thought the woman should practice more self-denial. Shulsky replied: "There's nothing wrong with self-denial when a person is building a fund with which to insure one's comfortable old age. But when one arrives at that age, it's time to be comfortable. If that includes spending some money on luxuries and little extras which one denied oneself during the years of accumulation, I say, go to it!"

He further explained how numerous senior citizens tightly grasp every penny. It was something they had learned to do following the Great Depression. They continue saving, even though they are financially secure. There's a time to sprint, a time to jog, and a time to walk. The passage of years, the changes in the world, and the incentives in our hearts should dictate the time for each. As we move from the old age of youth into the youth of old age, we need to monitor more than the passage of years. A variety of adjustments are called for. If we don't voluntarily change, the changes will be forced on us. Then we'll find ourselves rebelling and fighting the realities we can not escape. It's best to look ahead and plan for the next phase of the journey. It will help us to accept it when it comes.

The older we grow, the more we should try to solve our problems by wisdom rather than by muscle. Those who can not make that adjustment may be denying reality. Yet, wisdom and introspection are necessary at any age. Plato, the brilliant Greek philosopher of the fourth century B.C., referred to thinking as the "talking of the soul with itself." That is the way to wisdom and it helps us discover the right tempo for our daily living.

We easily associate physical activity with accomplishment because it's observable. The eye is impressed with physical motion and the sounds of activity touch the ear. And then we called it progress. Mental activity is of a different nature, and incidentally much more difficult than the physical. It's more stressful, more demanding, and often less satisfying. It also requires a lot of time. I'm sure many would not believe that.

I well remember those days in college when

I would spend four hours in serious study, usually before exams. I'd end up more tired and hungry than when I did physical labor. The body may appear to be at rest but the mind can be racing for a deadline. It's grasping for concepts, assembling them, understanding their meaning, and committing them to memory. That takes a lot of energy and leaves one very tired. It's as though we are mentally running a hard mile. Sometimes that's called for. Then we must lessen the pace again.

A reasonable pace to follow gives assurance of personal survival in the midst of our numerous activities. The word "pace" comes from the Latin "passus," meaning a step, or literally "the stretching out of the feet." This walking step is normally a stride of about two and one half feet. To walk in double time, means to stretch your stride to three feet. Every step we take is a reminder that long journeys are accomplished by small steps. We shouldn't jump to our conclusions, but walk to them step by step.

Mahatma Gandhi understood there was a different pace for every race. He could be fast and furious in his pursuit of political objectives for the sake of justice in his country. But just as suddenly he could stop, make a complete about-face, and calmly begin to meditate. He would become quiet and withdrawn within himself.

In America, we have a love-affair with the fast pace. It may be a track star, a football player making a touchdown run, an Indy car racer, a speedboat or fighter-jet pilot. Someone is always chasing a record and trying to rewrite history to the cheering encouragement of countless excited spectators. It seems like the natural thing to do. Yet, we can be too caught up in these things and neglect the inner journey which leads to true personal fulfillment. One of Gandhi's famous quotes is: "There is more to life than increasing its speed."

8

DISCIPLINE — A WAY OF LIFE

The ancient Greeks were known for their many excellent qualities of mind and body. They excelled in learning and physical achievements. One virtue they valued very highly, was that of discipline. It governed the lives of their famous philosophers Socrates, Plato, and Aristotle. It pushed their scholars to excel in thought and precise expression. The old saying is, "The Greeks had a word for everything." Discipline was the key element in their successful athletic events which gave us the name and origin of the modern Olympic games. It controlled the conduct of their armies and enabled Alexander the Great to conquer his vast territories.

In the midst of a people recognized for their national discipline, one man is especially remembered for carrying the concept to the ultimate. His name is Diogenes, known simply as a philosopher of ancient Greece. Born about 412 B.C., Diogenes became a member of the Cynic School of Philosophy. The Cynics taught that peoples' lives should be governed by self-control and they should be completely free of all desires for pleasures and material things. Diogenes adhered to this very strict life-style, and even in Cynic circles he was known as an extremist.

A crude, primitive shelter was his home and he walked the streets barefooted. Diogenes openly denounced riches and honors, and said there was no advantage in a noble birth. The only worthwhile goal to pursue, he said, was a virtuous life. Nothing was more valuable. Tradition tells us that he was often seen in the city of Athens carrying a lighted lantern. When he would meet a stranger, he would hold the lantern to the person's face with the comment, "I'm looking for an honest man."

Diogenes was a contemporary of Alexander the Great, and very much admired by the illustrious general. One day Alexander came to visit Diogenes and found him sunning himself. The powerful military leader stood in his presence and asked if there was anything he could do for him. Diogenes replied: "Yes, would you please move out of my sunlight?" His needs were the most basic and he wished to keep them that way. Alexander is reported to have remarked: "If I were not Alexander, I would like to be Diogenes."

We don't know if Diogenes was a happy man, but there's no mistaking the fact that he was disciplined. He had a way of thinking and acting which he, as a philosopher, had formulated and put into practice in his own life. He was so convinced of its correctness, he wanted to teach it to everyone he met.

Discipline has a variety of meanings, one of which has a negative connotation. Often we think of it as a type of punishment for doing wrong. Whether physical punishment or deprivation, discipline is frequently viewed as a pain inflicted to give assurance that some offense will not be repeated. The teacher disciplines a student because the student has been disrupting the class. If the student is deprived of playground time, he or she will think twice before disrupting class again. The hope behind the discipline is that it will lead to better class participation lest the punishment be repeated.

There is a very different and more positive meaning to discipline, one which is truer to its definition and certainly more attractive. It has to do with "learning." A disciple is a learner; a disciplined person is one who has learned how to live. In this sense, discipline implies a way of life, a conviction about what is best, and a dedication to adhere to it. The extremism of Diogenes is not advocated, but we should have our personal convictions and pursue them. Discipline is a common sense approach to daily life, ruled by reason rather than the emotion of the moment. It's a carefully thought-out plan to follow in those times when we would otherwise be in doubt. Discipline, in this fuller and deeper sense, instills an order and confidence in our lives as nothing else can.

The word "discipline" actually comes from the term "disciple," that is, "one who follows another" in person or in doctrine. The biblical disciples were those "disciplined people" who freely chose to follow the Master. When they could not literally follow him, they followed his teachings. They had their basic principles already charted for them. Circumstances would change each day and many times during the day, yet the established plan was there to guide them.

Living a disciplined life, in a negative sense, may seem like we are confined to a mental and physical straitjacket. We don't have room for spontaneity, fun, or adventure. Discipline is envisioned as something imposed on us to restrict our freedom or remove it entirely. Who wants to live like that? Nobody! Not even Diogenes. A positive discipline does exactly the opposite. It promotes our freedom, enhances our fun, creates a sense of adventure, and enables us to have true enjoyment. Our biggest problems result, not from using the good things of this earth, but from our over-using them. That, in reality, is not using but abusing. We should taste, sample, and enjoy all aspects of the wonders about us without expecting too much from them. Discipline provides us with a balanced and correct expectation.

Take diet for example. If we could learn the foods which are best for our health and the amounts we should eat, then we could establish our own discipline or plan of eating, realizing that we freely choose it, that it is long-range, and that it's for the sake of pursuing a healthy life-style. Such discipline will produce unbelievable results which will continue to delight us. It will enable us to control our weight, feel better, avoid being uncomfortably stuffed, make us more confident and, in fact, truly happier. Discipline helps us understand that contentment is found not in the food but within ourselves. When we voluntarily limit our needs, then we have more appreciation of what we already have. We all realize, for example, that the consumption of more food does not produce more elation.

Good health, not food, makes us feel good. Good health is one of our most prized possessions. It's often said: "If you have your health you have everything." We can't do our work very well if we don't feel well. Everyone's degree of physical health is either strengthened or weakened, largely depending on their daily choices. This is especially true in an area where we have maximum control — our diet. The food we consume both gives us the energy to perform our duties and builds up our strength to combat disease. Since diet depends on personal decisions and is basic to good health, then obviously, we need to make intelligent choices in this area. Recognizing our need for divine guidance, let us pray for help.

A Prayer For Dieters

Lord, give me strength that I may not fall
Into the clutches of cholesterol,
At polyunsaturates I'll never mutter
For the road to Hell is paved with butter.
And cake is cursed and cream is awful
And Satan is hiding in every waffle.

Beelzebub is a chocolate drop
And Lucifer is a lollipop.
Teach me the evils of hollandaise,
Of pasta and globs of mayonnaise
Of crisp, fried chicken from the South,
Lord, if you love me, shut my mouth.

The verse is anonymous, but the author has well expressed the struggle we all face. Food is one of life's biggest "flirts," always enticing us to indulge ourselves more than we ought. Self-discipline can help us avoid the "yoyo effect" in dieting. When we resolutely say, "Enough," the message is understood and observed. Very soon it becomes easier to limit our choices and amounts of food.

What is said of diet can easily be applied to most other areas of our lives. We don't have total control over the air we breathe and it may not be as pure as we would like. We can't stop breathing, but we can make some health-centered decisions and stop inhaling our own smoke-filled air. If we have a smoking habit and are convinced our health would be better if we stopped, then we're ready for a plan. Write it down, think it through, ask advice, set a date, and put it into effect. You might fail, maybe several times, but you've got a plan to follow. Eventually you'll get it. When you do, you'll find many unexpected benefits. You will also greatly benefit other people who will no longer be forced to breathe air polluted by your smoke.

We alone are personally responsible for controlling our alcohol consumption. Some say a drink a day is O.K., even beneficial. Others might debate that. Each person must decide what's best for them. The proper way to act requires a certain amount of discipline. For some, that may require a little help from their friends. The important thing is to have a plan and stick to it.

The acceptance of illegal drugs or the rejection of their use must also be dictated by personal self-discipline. Unquestionably, the rejection of their use on the part of many would improve our lives and our world in a very short time.

Each person must confront his or her own sexual desires and not allow a healthy attraction to become an abnormal addiction. When it comes to sex, many throw discipline to the wind, living by the motto "more is better." Experience shows the practice of multiple sexual partners does not lead to sexual fulfillment. To believe it does is to pursue a dangerous myth. Actually, it leaves one less fulfilled. Sex can easily get out of control. It can become an appetite gone berserk which feeds on everything it sees. Eventually it is satisfied by nothing. Lacking discipline, sex can turn vicious and deadly. Sexual crimes often dominate the news. It is ironic to realize that the drive meant to give life can produce so much death.

It's within our power to make numerous decisions which impact on our personal health and happiness. It's too dangerous to live without a plan, for no one is smart enough, or strong enough, to make major life decisions on the spur of the moment. It's especially hazardous to be without discipline when we are pressured by strong emotional feelings.

It would be ludicrous to think that a certain discipline alone could protect us from every disease, injury or physical failure. We need the helps and skills of others, especially those in the medical profession. Many predispositions are hereditary such as for heart disease, cancer, etc., but we have also inherited unique strengths. Our conduct can alter both for better or worse. All our genes need to be given the best fighting chance possible.

Even if we don't want to practice discipline for ourselves, we must do it for others. We need to provide a healthy environment for all those who can not yet practice discipline for themselves, namely our children born and unborn.

Does it not make a lot of sense to have a maintenance plan for our physical health? If we have one for our cars, trucks, tractors, refrigerators and copy machines, we certainly should have one for ourselves. Good health is not an accident.

The Bible say, "Physician, heal yourself." The same words are addressed to the "doctor" in each of us. The term "to heal" means to make whole. When our minds and bodies work together, with a sensible, long-range plan of discipline, the better, smarter, healthier and happier we will be.

9

A SELECTIVE MENTAL DIET

For many years I enjoyed the talks of the radio commentator Earl Nightingale. His program entitled *Our Changing World* was always innovative and inspirational. One presentation I especially remember addressed the subject of dieting based on the spiritual teachings of that outstanding scientist and philosopher, Emmet Fox. The diet proposed by Mr. Fox was not the ordinary type, but a 30-day diet for the mind. The objective was to achieve a well-conditioned mind in the same manner one pursues a disciplinary program for the body. Although Emmet Fox died in 1951, his thoughts are thoroughly contemporary and I found this idea especially exciting.

We normally don't think of the mind as an eater, but in reality it consumes a variety of impressions every day. Each day, in fact, the mind feeds on thousands of concepts and images. Some of these "mental foods" are healthy and bring needed nourishment to our lives. Other concepts and images are mental "junk foods." They are the cognitive sweets, fats and cholesterol which a healthy mind would want to avoid. All the concepts which we mentally digest, whether large portions or small nibbles, are assimilated into the mainstream of our inner lives. They become a part of us.

Emmet Fox suggests we do not feed our minds any negative thoughts, on any subject, for an entire period of 30 days. This he called "a selective mental consumption of ideas." He says the practice will enable us to improve our attitude and our performance.

Is a 30-day diet of only positive ideas a real possibility? We might close our eyes to the destructive and disheartening ills around us but it's more difficult to close our minds. There are many unwanted elements in the world and if we try to deny their existence, we are living in a state of self-deception. Yet it is possible to acknowledge the existence of evil and other negatives without being manipulated by them. They may be presented to us but we need not accept them. Freedom to choose is still our prerogative.

Restaurant menus inform the public of the wide variety of available foods, but the customers must make the choices. We make our selections according to what we like, or think will be most beneficial to our health. Most of us as adults would resent someone ordering for us without our consent. And we would be especially upset if another selected a food for us which we explicitly said we did not want. That same right of personal selection is ours when it concerns the ideas and ideals we choose to take into our minds. If the old maxim is true "We are what we eat," it is even more realistic to believe that we are what we think. A diet of negative, depressing and selfish thoughts can work havoc to our spirit, as truly as too much salt, sugar or fat can affect our physical fitness. In both cases we deteriorate, to some degree, in our overall sense of well-being.

When someone is acting strangely, we might inquire, "What's irking you?" Wouldn't we be surprised to hear the reply, "I'm suffering from an acute case of spiritual indigestion, which was caused by some negative ideas I swallowed last night." Most likely we don't think in those terms, but perhaps we should. Imagine what quality conversations we would have if we gave as much concern to our thought choices, as we do to the food we choose to eat.

Mental junk foods can be picked up on every street corner. Wherever we go, we can find them. They are available in all forms of the media, in everyday conversations and private thoughts. There will always be a line of willing volunteers, anxious to pour all the latest, morbid and sordid material into our ears. From there it easily flows into the blood stream of our inner existence. This mental junk food might seem appetizing and titillating at first, but later it can become the source of painful indigestion. When unwanted ideas are being offered, remember you choose the response. You can accept with smiling approval. Or you can promptly resist, as you might decline a juicy morsel of deep fried rattle-snake. If it seems like the wrong food for your mental diet, don't eat it.

We might surprise an anxious donor of un-wanted gossip with the words, "No thanks, my psyche is already upset. I must be very selective about my mental consumption." The fear is, a steady diet of hate, violence, and selfishness will eventually make us into what the menu offers.

On the positive side, a steady and consistent diet of hope, kindness, gentleness, and concern for others can turn us into better people with higher motives and loftier ideals. The thoughts we think, more than the food we eat, shape us into what we really are. The body knows what is best for it and responds accordingly. Some medi-cines it can accept and some it can't. The mind, even more so, knows what is best and what is needed. In the pursuit of healthiness, we owe both body and mind the best diets we can pro-vide. It's exciting to envision all the wonderful achievements which could result from a positive 30-day mental diet.

We may be searching for meaning, happi-ness and fulfillment in all the wrong places and in all the wrong ways. These are not found in be-littling others to exalt ourselves. They are not found in exotic vacations and glittering posses-sions. True meaning and genuine happiness must begin inwardly and expand outwardly. Nothing external can make us happy if we are discon-tented at the center of our being. What can be more central to our very existence than our personal thoughts and ideas?

The truck commercial for the Ford Ranger says it well: "The toughest competition we have is ourselves." We should be as demanding on ourselves as we are on others. Some require more of themselves than of others. We can identify those individuals as the ones who excel. If we require less of ourselves than others, that too becomes evident — on the negative side. Imagine what radical, internal improvements could take place within, simply by making an effort to exercise more control of our lives.

All people have their own personal set of problems, which are varied and many. Yet, one's individual attitude is often the epicenter of the problem. A 30-day mental diet of positive concepts could radically improve a listless attitude. Give it a try. What do you have to lose except those unwanted, negative, heavy thoughts which needlessly weigh you down and make you miserable?

It's always so easy to join the crowd, to blame others in the flow of uncharitable conversation, and feel superior by stepping on a competitor. The advice is often given to avoid bitter words about another, for later on we may have to eat those words.

One of the qualities which made Abraham Lincoln so great was his ability to see the brighter, more positive side of every situation. He often took a verbal beating without becoming bitter.

Lincoln refused to mentally chew or swallow what would deter him from a healthy inner life. Therefore, he could be free of bitterness and a desire for revenge.

In 1850, Edwin Stanton, an Ohio lawyer, requested the legal services of Abraham Lincoln who, at the time, was a rising young legal giant from Springfield, Illinois. When the two men met in Cincinnati, Stanton treated Lincoln coldly and ignored him during the case they were trying. It is said that Stanton "stage whispered" to a group around him, "I won't associate with such a long-armed gawky ape as that." Twelve years later Lincoln was President of the United States and for the position of Secretary of War he appointed Edwin Stanton. It was a clear sign Lincoln had not taken to heart the offensive conduct of Stanton nor digested his bitter words. Three years later, Stanton stood at the bedside of the dying president, weeping like a baby at the loss of his most dear friend, Abraham Lincoln.

We can avoid being dominated inwardly by a depressive exterior environment, but it requires a constant and monumental effort. Lofty ideals alone will not lead us to this worthy achievement. We may begin with a grand plan, but without daily practice, our efforts will soon become as futile as a fraternity football team after their third case of beer. Too often, we simply are unwilling to make the sustained effort necessary for a new way of thinking. The whole idea becomes nothing more than a passing thought, rather than a way of life.

The famous Greek, Epictetus said, "It's not your problems that will destroy you but the way you look at them." We often complain that modern day society has taken control of our lives. There are rules and regulations for practically every area of our existence. We have little to say about government, health care, taxes, media, etc. You wonder if we would make significant improvements even if we had real power to do so. I make that statement because we do have control over our thoughts and other personal areas of our lives and we see the mess we often make. Since we don't like to acknowledge our failures, we easily lay the blame on neighbors, politicians, government and even God. If we are so responsible minded, why don't we exhibit more power and control over our own lives?

One area where we often excel is making excuses for ourselves. That we do well. The litany is long: I'm tired, offended, discouraged, burned out, etc. Remember, you first must have an original fire before you can have a burnout. A fire also is an eater, which requires proper fuel. If we want it to continue burning, we must feed it the "right diet." If we feed our fire the wrong material it will soon die. Positive, affirming concepts will do for our spirits what summer-dried pine branches will do for a fire. The flame in your fireplace is beautiful and warming only because you give it the right diet and proper care. No less is required for the flame which lives within us.

Avoid the quick fix, the instant result and the immediate gratification, which have become the trademarks of our times. Someone said we can't be a capitalist without capital. Nor can we have a calm heart, a peaceful mind, and broad view of life if we are so narrow-minded that our ears touch. Those who are really concerned about making a better world don't begin by marching down the streets of Washington D.C., but by reforming themselves. Then they can be on display for others to see what can be accomplished and informed as to how it can be done.

The guiding principle is: What goes into any project or endeavor is what will eventually come out of it. What we digest in the stomach will eventually reach the blood stream. From there, it will influence the entire system. What we digest in our minds will enter the mainstream of our thoughts. The achievement of a goal, therefore, requires more than wishful thinking. The plan must be directed. The current saying is, "If you continue to do what you've been doing, you'll continue to get what you've been getting." If you don't like what you've been getting, then the formula must change.

If we are convinced we have the power and ability to change for the better, then we're ready to begin. Soon we'll see positive results and realize we're not controlled by every passing whim. That will be an inspiration for continued efforts and further improvements. This newly discovered power will give us a mystical sense of experiencing the priceless. Journaling our thoughts and self-made rules can be very helpful to our mental and emotional attitudes. It enables us to see progress in the making.

An accomplished actor once made the comment, "The reason so many are thrilled with my performance is because I am not." The foes of self-improvement are living within us and around us. They may be hard to define and difficult to defeat but that makes the victory all the more satisfying.

10

LOOKING WITHIN
AND BEYOND

Dad: "Don't you think our daughter gets all
       her brains from me?"
Mom: "Probably, I still have all mine."

Where do we get our brains? We inherit
many qualities as color of eyes and hair, talents,
and a myriad of other characteristics from our
long line of ancestors. Where these various qualities originated, or how they came to be, remains
a mystery. We're always searching for more complete answers as to what and who we are and
what is the purpose and meaning of our lives.

Those who achieve success often say they
are not at peace. All of us probably agree, our
accomplishments don't bring that complete happiness which we once imagined. Life is a struggle
and everyone is confronted with unexpected
difficulties and discouragements. Yet, we find
within ourselves hope and reason to persevere.

It is a long-standing tradition, we also look
outside ourselves for the meaning and fulfillment

of our existence. The human heart has inherited an instinctive desire to search for some mysterious being or power that holds the key to our existence and self-understanding. This elusive, hidden power is always beyond our immediate grasp. We seek this unknown entity as a type of mystical Rosetta stone wherein we might translate life's deepest mysteries. This elusive enigma and envisioned force may be called by different titles; but for many, the name is God.

God is called Almighty, Divine, Supreme, All-Knowing and Sovereign of the Universe. God is envisioned as holding the answers to those ever pressing questions about the beginning and ultimate meaning of life. How do we channel our efforts to find God, to understand the ways of God, or even to know if there is a God?

There was a time when I was absolutely nothing. I'm sure of that. I often puzzle over my beginning. I had to come from somewhere. Parents, of course, but that begins the long road back through history to the original beginning. With uncertainty I also look in the other direction. Is it not logical that, in the future, I may return to absolutely nothing? Is there really a life after death? If so, what is it and where is it?

It's fascinating to try to explain our own, individual conception and birth. We know that, at the time of our conception, hundreds of thousands other possible persons could have been conceived instead. And we would never have existed. Someone else would have been born in our place. That individual would have had a whole different set of characteristics and may even have been of the opposite sex. Was it pure chance one particular sperm met one particular egg which resulted in the person we call ourselves, or was that directed in some way by another power?

Our origins and destinies are profound and intriguing but there are so many more unsolved questions around us. Why, for example, should a young, innocent, loving person die from a disease, injury or the violence of another? What is the purpose of this world? Or does it have one? We have a most friendly planet as our home. The ground produces food, the clouds filter the sun and hold the heat. The world offers us a wonderful life. Here we have a remarkable home. These ideal conditions seem not to exist on the other planets we have studied. Thus the entire solar system and the magnitude of space are absolutely mind boggling. Does this one mighty power — God — control it all?

We hear people speaking about God's will but that's another profound mystery. Many believe God holds the solution to every mystery, thus God is the answer. Yet the existence and nature of God is one of the deepest mysteries. We, therefore, use a mystery to solve a mystery. Some of the very best minds in human history have ingeniously and prayerfully struggled with the concept and meaning of God. Only a few, nebulous insights have been produced. Thus the question remains: Who and what is God?

The most general dictionary definition of

God is "any of various beings, conceived of as supernatural, immortal and having power over the lives and affairs of people and the course of nature."

Religion is a bonding system by which we attempt to establish a connection or communication with God. The term religion is from the Latin (*re + ligare*), meaning to bind together. It has the same root as our term ligament, which ties together the bones and other parts of our bodies. This "spiritual ligament," attempts to tie together the human and the divine, the natural and the supernatural, creatures and creator. Beyond formal definitions, people have many personal interpretations of what religion is or should be.

It's commonly taught there are eleven major world religions and all have different ideas of God's nature and the manner in which one should be bonded. Many people profess Christianity, Judaism, or Islam. Some follow the "middle way" recommended by Buddhism. Others prefer the ethical teachings of Confucianism. Still others profess the Hindu belief expressed in the sacredness of all living things. These world religions have different terminology, but all seek the same ultimate truth. The Koran of Islam explains why and how to bind oneself to God. The Torah of Judaism and, in a unique way, the Gospels of Christianity explain why and how God binds himself to us.

Religion, like nationality, is characterized by its variety. We may belong to one of the denominations of Christianity, or to another of the world religions, or have no formal religion at all. Yet, there seems to be present within everyone a similar natural impulse which offers a common guiding light to make moral decisions and act in a responsible way.

The story is told of the U.S. golfer, Tommy Bolt, who was known for his graceful swing and quick temper. Once after missing six short putts he was absolutely furious. Looking at the sky he shook his fist saying: "Why don't you come down and fight like a man?"

Some say God controls every minute, thought, and action — like golf putts. Actually God is blamed for the missed ones; those made are the result of human skill. Others feel God exerts no influence on any happening in the world. God is remote, an impersonal being. As noted, many think there is no God to whom you can shake your fist or offer a prayer. That's where faith comes in. "Faith is confident assurance regarding things we hope for and firm conviction about the reality of things unseen" (Hebrews 11:1). It is an almost universal phenomenon. William Cummings said, "There are no atheists in foxholes." When times are difficult and the going gets rough, faith in God gives us reason to hope and inclines us to pray.

For those who would like to offer a simple but profound prayer, I would suggest using three ancient Hebrew words. The lips of Jesus formed and prayed these very words. We can do likewise, making the same sounds he did. We can't fathom his deep and all-embracing thoughts when he prayed these words, but we can imagine what they might have been and express our own. Regardless of the degree of influence you believe God has over you and various events, this prayer can be very meaningful. Find a quiet place, clear your mind of worries and center your thoughts on God.

Say ABBA. This is a very affectionate Hebrew term for father. It is literally translated as "daddy." It is the term Jesus told his disciples to use when they said the Lord's Prayer. As you speak this title, try to grasp what Abba must be — spirit, cloud-like, intelligent, in heaven, inside you, etc. Each time you consider a new or different concept of God you can repeat the term, "Abba." Picture yourself as a small child relating to your loving father in a very trusting way. You're not asking for any favors, nor lamenting any wrongs. You are simply reinforcing a gentle bonding between creator and created. You need not speak any other words, only pour forth the thoughts of your mind. It can become a mystical experience, a mind-to-mind encounter, mental telepathy. After lingering over the image of Abba for a few minutes, you then can move on to the second part of the prayer.

ALLELUIA. It is a very familiar Hebrew word. "Alleluia" means one is happy and rejoicing. Here, you can recall and picture the thousands of blessings in your life. There's the gift of life itself; then family and those who love you. "Alleluia" includes your successes, rewards, happy times, material blessings, hopes for the future and joys of every kind. For each of these, you can repeat "Alleluia" over and over. This second part of the Hebrew prayer can make you feel very fortunate and secure. You don't have all the money you want, or every desired material possession, but you are very rich. You have a wealth that far exceeds material things. This one word expresses your thanks and appreciation for all the good which has touched your life. It's a classy way of saying thanks for everything. This second part of the prayer helps you stop complaining about what you don't possess and appreciate what you do. It's difficult to exhaust all your alleluias.

AMEN is the final word of the prayer. It means "so be it." Amen to Abba. Amen to Alleluia. Amen to the entire spectrum of existence, both the pleasant and the painful. You're saying Amen to everything that is; especially those difficult realities and situations which you can't control. It's your acceptance prayer. Jesus had to speak his "Amens" to the Father many times. So must we.

Amen to my personal hurts and sicknesses, to my suffering loved ones. Amen to what I can't control, the accidents, injuries and deaths of people on the highways and in other areas. I can do nothing but accept them.

Amen to the fact that I am growing older, slowing down, and readjusting my life to this time and place. Those who pray their Amens sincerely, should become more accepting of their adverse situations. Amen does not mean I agree with all that is or that I easily tolerate it. It means my power is limited and I am forced to accept what I can not change.

Amen to all that was, is and will be. Alleluia to the blessings, too numerous to count or even imagine. Abba, to the divine, loving Father, the God of the universe.

Beyond these three meaningful and powerful words there's not much more to say in prayer. Sure, we could pour out a thousand petitions for desired favors or thanksgivings. We could lament over our personal sins and faults. We could beg for all the strength needed to face hardships. This is all done in the three words of the Hebrew Prayer.

Does God have any influence over golf putts, earthquakes, nuclear bombs or births of babies? I believe that his hand is in or behind everything that is or occurs even though I don't even begin to understand how or to what degree. I do know I have a home in the universe, but I'm not sure how I got here. My philosophy book says: "Every effect has a cause." I have my cause and my parents had theirs, and so it goes far back into the fog and night of history. I'm a little person in a tiny boat on the vast ocean of life and so are you.

When I've uttered my Abba, Alleluia and Amen, I am sure — again because of my faith — that I am heard. In the New Testament, Jesus was very clear about that: "Ask and you shall receive, seek and you will find, knock and it will be opened to you." We may not hear a voice responding, but we are assured that our thoughts have been heard by another who loves us and has promised in Scripture to provide us with all we truly need. It is my prayer. It is spoken with sincerity and when I've said it, I feel less isolated and better able to lean against the wind.

11

MORE QUESTIONS
THAN ANSWERS

William Somerset Maugham is remembered as a very brilliant man. Some of his accomplishments include the fact that, as a young man, he became a noted English novelist, an author of short stories, and an outstanding playwright. Since his father served as a British Embassy official in Paris where he was born, Maugham was knowledgeable in government matters, too.

Early in his career, the study of medicine attracted William to St. Thomas Hospital in London. There he completed most of the required courses to be a doctor. It was the literary calling, however, which won his heart and he never practiced medicine. Maugham's research, studies, observations and personal reflections made him a highly intellectual person.

Why do I tell you of this twentieth century Englishman? Simply to acknowledge his remarkable intelligence and to note a very significant statement he once made. Maugham said, "It wasn't until quite late in life that I discovered how easy it is to say, 'I don't know.'"

Perhaps we feel that such words should be spoken only by the uninformed, not by someone who is really intelligent. Wise individuals are expected to have the answers, or at least to be able to make some positive response to any question. Were the well-educated to say they didn't know, wouldn't their reputations for brilliance be in some way tarnished? No! Just the opposite is true.

Those who feel obliged to answer every question will often give wrong or incomplete information. When we have no explanation we should not try to make others believe we do. We may talk around a question, in an effort to sound knowledgeable, but people can easily recognize our stumbling confusion. It would be more honest to follow Maugham's observation and simply say, "I don't know." Our credibility would rise proportionately.

When you say you don't know something, that doesn't mean you've never thought about it or you don't have some opinion on the matter. You may, in fact, have pondered a question for a long time, considering every possible angle. To respond, "I don't know," in such a case may still be the most intelligent reply possible.

I've heard people brag about asking speakers questions they couldn't answer. If the speaker is a recognized expert on the subject, the questioner may get the false impression he's smarter than the expert. How foolish can we be? The speaker could ask a hundred more difficult queries and completely baffle the entire audience. It's no outstanding accomplishment to ask a tough question. It is a sign of genuine integrity at times, however, to say you don't know.

Alex Haley, who died in 1992, is remembered for his diligent research into his past family history. His famous work *Roots* made a profound impact on America and inspired many to investigate their own ancestral background. The story is told of Haley's uncle who was so proud of his education that he continually wore his Phi Beta Kappa key. It was displayed on a chain around his neck. Another of Haley's relatives, a lady who had a very practical bent, one day met his uncle. She saw the key and remarked: "Very pretty, but what does it unlock?"

The keys to our homes and cars are practical items, giving us a means of entry, but there are many locked doors to which there are no keys available. If those doors are to be unlocked someday, it will not be with a key of metal but with the key of knowledge. Mysterious possibilities exist, hidden deep within ourselves and others. Countless secrets are locked in nature and hidden in the earth and sky. Here locksmiths can not help us; we must rather turn to the teacher, to books and other sources of wisdom. We manage daily to unlock new secrets but at a very slow pace and one answer often brings more puzzling questions. When someone asks what's inside those doors, we therefore should never be hesitant to say, "I don't know."

Politicians are notorious for their vague and non-specific replies. They like to rephrase the question to fit their existing answers, rather than find the precise key to a particular problem. Their responses are often not answers but simply sound bites fashioned to please the media. "I don't know" is not one of their favorite phrases. It doesn't attract votes. But it should.

Walt Disney did a lot to help the world see and appreciate the secrets of the universe around us. He always informed in a captivating way. Disney once said, "I would rather entertain and hope people would learn, than try to teach and hope people would be entertained." Stories were his favorite teaching device. The story itself rarely presents a definite answer to a problem or mystery, but rather comments on it. It throws some light on the matter and does so in a pleasing manner.

The wise person is to be highly respected. Achievement in learning is one of the loftiest of human accomplishments. The prudent application of that knowledge is what we call wisdom. Wisdom has more clout than the billionaire's money, the athlete's strength, or the politician's popularity. Genuine wisdom can easily out duel and overcome any opposition. It opens the most baffling of mysteries and sheds light on the unknown future. We all have dozens of questions we would like to ask a person who is truly wise.

Can we become wisdom-centered people? We can certainly try. It doesn't matter where we start, we can all increase in this most precious quality of our lives. Here are a few ways to proceed.

Instead of always asking and depending on

others, learn to find your own answers. Consult the proper sources. There is no substitute for the LIBRARY. It's the "tallest" building in town, with many more "stories" than you can imagine. It should be one of your favorite buildings. Go to visit it often. Become acquainted with the reference books. Note the different kinds available and challenge them to produce the answers you seek. They will lead you to other books, articles and different sources. Always carry a pen and note-pad to record your new found knowledge. Then commit the material to memory and make it a part of you.

A book that should have high priority in your life is the dictionary. Have your own and use it everyday. When you see or hear words you like, but have never used, note their root meaning, verify their spelling, and make them yours. You do that by employing them immediately, in your daily vocabulary. Understanding the exact meaning of a word and using it correctly is a step up the ladder of learning. Most of our ideas are expressed through words. Think of words as your friends. Their origins, meanings, and distinctions can teach us a lot of things. Words can enable us to express ourselves precisely and to better understand when others speak to us.

Wisdom is even more precious than knowledge, but both are wonderful. Ask your dictionary to define them and show you how they differ. Knowledge can lead us to success or into trouble. We may acquire the knowledge to break the Pentagon computer code or assemble a powerful explosive. When police have to deal with a "smart" criminal, they have a big problem on their hands. Knowledge is great but it can both help and harm the common good. Wisdom, however, will never lead one into evil or dishonesty. We can never have too much wisdom. The more the better. Everyone benefits.

Common sense is a byproduct of wisdom. Without it we risk being ruled by superstition. How easy it is to attach certain powers to inanimate objects which can not possibly affect our lives. Don't you get irritated by those predatory "chain letters" and the fear they try to engender? Yet, because we don't have all the answers and do have fears, we easily fall prey to superstitions. The baseball player who hit two home runs yesterday insists on wearing the same socks when he takes the field today. Common sense says there is no connection and it's unfitting of intelligent people to think in those ways, but we sometimes do. Some mysteries will never be solved. Their scope and intensity are far beyond our powers to comprehend; still, we continue to question. It's in our nature. There are a million more questions than answers.

It is said that Teddy Roosevelt would often walk out into the night with some of his friends and search the heavens. He would talk about the stars, the galaxies with their millions of suns and the vastness of the Milky Way. After a time, it was his habit of saying, "Now I think we are small enough. Let's go to bed." Incidentally, it's good to have a pencil and pad near your bed. What has eluded you during the day, your subconscious mind may reveal to you in dreams.

When something is beyond our comprehension we do well to admire it without feeling we have to completely understand it. When it concerns outer space and the explanation of the solar system, we expect to hear many people say, "I don't know." Jane Taylor's little nursery rhyme says it all:

> "Twinkle, twinkle, little star
> *How I wonder* what you are,
> Up above the world so high
> Like a diamond in the sky."

It's easy to ask a thousand intelligent questions about the cosmos. The most informed astronomer could not provide answers to some. Even ordinary things are difficult to explain. What makes the wind blow? How does gravity work? Why is blood red? Of course there are some answers to these, and certain people have better explanations than others. But they also have their mysteries. The more complicated the entity, the more mystery surrounds it.

I remember reading a statement made by George Bernard Shaw. He must have had a difficult day with some people and found it impossible to explain their behavior. He said, "From the actions of humankind it seems to me as if this particular planet of ours must be the insane asylum for some other world." Shaw confirms what we all know. It's very difficult to imagine what the members of the human race will do next. We are thoroughly unpredictable. Who can understand us?

Shaw was one of those who are always looking for a better answer to basic questions. His plays and other writings continually address the social aspects of society. He believed in an evolution of the human race, as did Darwin. But what Darwin called a "Biological Evolution," Shaw called "Creative Evolution." The difference was that Darwin credited everything to change and environment while Shaw allowed for intelligence and purpose. The question of evolution versus creation still continues to be debated today. The empirical sciences tell us painfully little about our primeval origins and less about our eternal destiny. They provide us with many questions, much speculation, and few definitive answers. For some answers we must turn to faith and divine revelation.

Art Linkletter once said the best interviews are people older than 80 and younger than 10. "Both groups speak sincerely. The children don't know and the elderly don't care." William Somerset Maugham encourages us not to wait until we are 80 before we speak sincerely. He lived to be 91 but didn't learn to be completely open until "late in life." How can we be more open and honest in what we believe and say? I don't know. I'm still trying. I wish you well.

I can only say, question everything you can. Consult your books to see what others have written. Listen to those you respect. Enjoy the company of thinkers. They may not be consummate conversationalists but they are almost always enlightening. Think and rethink on your own. Seek to fill your life with real quality. To some questions you will be able to supply the desired information. In regard to other problems, be proud to say, "I don't know." Don't be afraid to acknowledge your sense of awe and reverence when confronted with the mysteries of the universe. Then others will trust your wisdom and you will have credibility.

12

TRUST THE TRUTH

There is a story told about a kind old rabbi who lived in Germany before the outbreak of World War Two. He was loved by all who knew him. His popularity, however, was resented by the Nazis and they set about to remove him from the scene. Their plot was to bribe a beautiful young lady to bring about his downfall. She was to visit the rabbi on some pretense and then publicly accuse him of having molested her. The sequence developed as planned and the shocked rabbi and his many friends loudly and consistently declared his innocence. He, nonetheless, was taken to court for trial.

In spite of all the devious efforts of the Gestapo, the jury could not find him guilty. The trial lingered on and the rabbi continued to proclaim his innocence with loud prayer, expressing his deep trust in God. Over and over he repeated, "God will deliver me." Finally, he was asked if he would trust his God enough to leave the decision of his case to chance.

The judge explained that two slips of paper would be placed in a box, one marked "Guilty," the other "Innocent." The rabbi would choose one and that would be his fate, whether favorable or not. The rabbi agreed, saying God would certainly deliver him from this false accusation. The judge personally wrote "Guilty" and "Innocent" on the papers, placed them in a box and sealed it. "The fate of the rabbi," he said, "will be decided in the morning when he draws one of the papers." The rabbi smiled with confidence.

During the night the Gestapo approached the judge and offered him — as was their customary tactic — an enormous bribe. The judge was asked to unseal the box, remove the "Innocent" paper and make both of them read "Guilty." The judge accepted the corrupt bribe and did as requested. "Now," the Nazis whispered, "we've got the rabbi. He will be condemned. There is no way out."

The next morning the court convened and the sealed box was delivered directly from the safe. The rabbi confidently stepped forward and drew his lot. Momentarily he held the paper in his hand without opening it. Then, still without examining it, he suddenly thrust the paper into his mouth, chewed and swallowed it. The court gasped in astonishment. "Why I did that," the rabbi said, "I don't know." He explained it seemed like God had told him to. Then he addressed the court, assuring everyone that there was no need for confusion. "To determine my verdict," he said, "simply examine the other paper left in the box. See what it says."

The judge had no choice but to hold up, for

all to see, the paper marked "Guilty." The towns-people loudly applauded and the rabbi shouted, "I chose the 'Innocent' one. God has spared my life for I am innocent."

Our trials in life may not be as dramatic, but the same principle applies nonetheless. We need to trust the truth, for eventually the truth will tri-umph. It will enlighten us and expose falsehood and deceit. We applaud the truth and strive to live by it.

Mark Twain said, "When in doubt tell the truth." If you don't always tell the truth you should have a very good memory. We speak of the truth as if it were perfectly clear to everyone and as if all have the exact same idea of what it is. Truth, however, can be a nebulous concept and have a variety of meanings to different people. This can be an eye-opener, especially to most chil-dren. When understood correctly, it can lead to personal growth and maturation.

The ancient question of Pilate still haunts people today, "What is truth?" In my philosophy class in college the professor often emphasized the basic distinction between objective and sub-jective truth. After these many years I can still hear him saying: "Objective truth is the way something exists in reality. Subjective truth is the way something exists in your mind." For in-stance: Tom had a car accident in a busy intersec-tion. The light was red and Tom went through it. Tom knew it was red but he was in a hurry and took a chance. He admitted he was in the wrong. That which was in reality and that which was in

Tom's mind were the same. Objective and subjective truth agreed.

If however, Tom really thought the light was green he was following his subjective truth, which now differs from the objective truth. The light in reality was red. Tom did not violate his conscience but he did violate the traffic laws and he was guilty. He was objectively guilty but not subjectively so, that is, in his conscience. The fine, however, was still given, since the law must follow the objective truth.

Isn't it amazing how people interpret events from their subjective point of view? A policeman is quoted as saying: "After you have heard two eye witness accounts of an auto accident, you begin to wonder about history."

When we apply these same principles to our way of thinking and judging our own lives and the world around us, we can all say we are following the truth even though we act in many different ways. People may contradict each other, yet claim to be speaking the truth, the truth, that is, as they see it. Not only is this possible, it is in fact quite common. Subjective truth can mean many different things.

Our task is to see the reality of any situation as clearly as possible, and without bias. The closer we get to the objective truth, the better off we will be.

One person might say, I follow the truth in everything I do and, therefore, my life is good and quite simple. That sounds impressive. Indeed, it's a wonderful way to live, but it's not that easy.

Knowing and living the objective truth can be very hard to do at times.

There is objective morality and subjective morality. Some would say there is no such thing as objective morality, it's all subjective, for morality concerns human actions and all human actions are subjective. True. There is always a subjective element in every human action. But there is also an objective element to every human action. Objective here refers to a norm: the common way of acting by most people. Laws are a codified reflection of the norm as are moral principles based on the Golden Rule or the Ten Commandments. In any group of people we can expect to have a variety of opinions regarding what is right and what is wrong, what is permissible and what is unacceptable in society. If everyone is thinking the same way, some are probably not thinking at all. That brings us to the problem of how to deal fairly with all. How do we make laws to govern everyone and mandate punishments when these laws are violated?

The best we can do, is strive for the objective truth in our judgments and use that as the basic guide for our society. The truth, in other words, will never be perfectly clear in itself and we, therefore, will seldom have unanimous agreement. For that reason there needs to be patience among people and not condemnation at the slightest provocation. When people think, speak and act in a way different from us, they are not less conscientious. They may be as sincere as we are or even more.

I read a California business man's list of "truths" by which he tries to live. He had these printed on the back of his business card:

"The greatest sin is fear of the future.
The greatest mistake is giving up.
The most satisfying experience is doing
    your duty first.
The best action is keeping the mind clear
    and judgment sound.
The biggest fool is the person who lies to
    himself.
The most certain thing in life is change.
The greatest joy is being needed.
The cleverest person is the one who does
    what he thinks is right.
The greatest opportunity is the next one.
The great thought is God.
The greatest achievement is victory over
    self."

We have truths by which we live, but most are not recorded. I suggest you formulate your own list of guidelines, by which you live. Commit them to paper: read them, revise them, and live them. It's easy to allow our views to be influenced by cliches which are not really our own. Our lives and precious time on earth are too valuable to let them be ruled and guided by the bumper stickers and ten-second media bites.

Sometimes the truths by which we live and work don't tell the whole story but they are useful nonetheless. There is an old adage, for ex-

ample, among fishermen explaining the best conditions for a successful catch: "Wind from the
west, fish bite best. Wind from the east, fish bite
least." Many claim the old maxim has proven itself on countless occasions. A biologist will tell
you that the west wind makes better fishing because it's generally warmer and brings the insects
upon which the fish like to feed. Regardless, such
sayings reflect the wisdom of the ages passed
down from generation to generation regarding
the mysteries of the sea where most is hidden
from our view.

Much also is hidden within the lives of
people we meet. We normally see only surface
deeds without any explanation. That is why we
can so easily misjudge. We think of ourselves as
being very dependable, honest and caring. Why,
then, do we often think of others as insincere or
undependable, and not as dedicated as they
should be? If we knew the truth, the people we
often censure may be more trustworthy than we.
It's tempting but very reckless for us to be judg-
mental.

The less we know of others, the easier it is
to be suspicious of their motives. In his poem *To
Know All Is to Forgive All*, Nixon Waterman writes:

> "If I knew you and you knew me
> If both of us could clearly see,
> And with an inner sight divine
> The meaning of your heart and mine
> I'm sure that we would differ less
> And clasp our hands in friendliness;

Our thoughts would pleasantly agree
If I knew you and you knew me."

Diplomats use the phrase today, "Trust but verify." It's their version of accepting the subjective truth as a beginning but demanding to see the objective truth before the deal is made. People who have different views are not to be feared, as long as they are consistent. It's the "chameleons" who give us trouble. Truth for them is whatever is popular at the moment.

Truth, to some is not reality, but what they try to make others think is real. Our age has been characterized as the epoch of illusion, where slogans are considered solutions and rhetoric is fact. The Roman statesman Seneca counseled his people to be patient, even when angry because "Time discovers truth." The world is in need of honest people who are unafraid to speak the truth in love. Harry Truman once said: "People say I give them hell. I only tell them the truth and they think it's hell." The truth is precious and needs to be treated always with the utmost respect. It is the truth which will set us free.

13

THE FLIP SIDE OF LIFE

The parents of a five year old girl bought a colorful jigsaw puzzle of the world for her. They knew their daughter was too young to put it together, but thought she could learn names and locations of various countries. The little girl was pleased with her gift and began searching for the matching pieces.

One afternoon, after she had been playing with the puzzle, her mother found her asleep and the pieces all interlocked in place. She was totally amazed and wondered how her daughter had done it. When the girl awoke, her mother asked how she had managed to assemble it. The girl explained that one of the pieces had fallen on the floor and landed with the world's side down. On the back side of this piece was a picture of a man's nose. Curiously, she examined the back sides of other pieces, and to her amazement saw eyes, hands and ears. The girl realized there was a man's picture painted on the back side of the world, so she turned all the pieces of the puzzle over and put together the man. "Everyone knows," she told her mother, "how a man goes together." When she flipped the assembled puzzle over, the whole world was also all together.

Don't we often forget there are two sides to every situation, like that jigsaw puzzle? There's a picture on both sides. How we assemble one side will likewise affect the other. If something is out of place in the human picture, it will cause the world to be askew. When individuals are well ordered, the world automatically follows. We can not abuse human life — our own or others, and expect the world to remain intact. Nor can the world be abused without causing an adverse effect on the people who occupy it.

The more we indulge in selfish pursuits, the more we divide people and tear apart our world. A chemical company may release toxic gases into the air at night, thinking nobody will know. But some people will breathe that air, and to some extent, it will affect their health. We pollute our streams, rivers and lakes because they're convenient dumping places and we might not get caught. The drinking water, as well as the fish, become affected and again peoples' health and lives are harmed. But the reverse is likewise true. The day I take the time to gather up one bag of litter is the day I make the world a better place in which to live.

Imagine the high quality of life we all could have if everyone felt obliged to do good deeds to help rather than to harm others. If individuals would improve their life-styles, society would automatically benefit. The old saying is: "If you're not part of the solution, you're part of the problem." When we limit ourselves to only one point of view, our own, we become part of the problem.

Our opinion may seem best. That's why we defend it, but we must be honest enough to admit other people have different opinions. They are equally convinced their viewpoints are correct. So how can we work in harmony that the world may be one? There needs to be a cooperative unity and sense of tolerance between people. There will always be a wide variety of opinions among different individuals and groups. It's an absolute must, for we are born differently. Yet, variety need not be divisive. We can live in peaceful unity without demanding uniformity. It's the only way to be at peace with the world and with each other.

It's a delicate road to walk between caring for self while respecting all others. The laws of justice and equity are to be observed in dealing with both. The judge and jury in court cases constantly face this dilemma. If the guilty person is not punished, then an innocent person is wronged and society suffers. If an innocent person is found guilty, which may happen more often than we'd like to admit, severe injustice is done to that individual and to all society. No one benefits from injustice, even those who seem to, for if anyone's human rights are violated, all human rights to some extent are transgressed. One wrong decision made by one person has many negative and hurtful results because every decision affects more than one person.

When someone runs a red light, that person is affecting those who are on the other side of the intersection. Their rights and lives are threatened and that causes anger and often revenge. When a robber steals money at gun point, he may be thinking only of how the money will benefit him. He may never consider the hellish fears and nightmares he will cause for the one who has the gun shoved in his face. He's unconcerned about the flip side of his devious deed.

An intoxicated driver hits someone on the sidewalk. Maybe he had a good time at the bar and a real thrill ride but on the other side of the puzzle is a dead pedestrian. That person is a parent, spouse, relative and friend to many other people. For them, the pieces of the puzzle will never completely fit together again. Time will never totally heal the hurt; the damage is irreversible. To every action there is a reaction, many of which we will never know.

Sensitivity is a marvelous quality to possess, for it makes us more aware of what we do, and how our actions may affect the lives of others. Even our thoughts are not entirely private for they eventually are manifested in deeds. So the more we control our minds, the better our external acts will be, for ourselves and others. When thoughts are translated into deeds, they either help or hurt others who live on the flip side of our life.

One of the most important precepts of the

Bible is found in Matthew 7:12. It's the "Big Rule" of the New Testament. This one guideline of conduct is so precious and valuable it's called "Golden." The "Golden Rule" tells us very clearly and very directly to remember those who are on the flip side: "Do unto others what you would have them do unto you." We have the power to make the existence of others miserable through our narrow-minded, uncaring attitude. But the opposite is also true. Dare we imagine the incomparable peace and blessed security all could experience by a collective decision to be more aware and caring of other peoples' feelings? Starting tomorrow we could literally change the face of the earth if everyone would begin to observe Matthew 7:12.

The holistic view of life is constantly emphasized today. It's a principle that a person or organization has a reality which is independent of and more than the sum total of its parts. The total person or organization is the ultimate. All the parts of one's life must contribute to the good of the whole. That, too, is an attempt to place all things in order. Some areas of my life must be disciplined and denied in order to give other areas a chance to excel or simply survive. This in turn will benefit the total person.

We can not be narrow-minded even about ourselves. I run, for example, to exercise my heart and lungs, but holistically I must not overdo it or I risk injuring my ankles or my knees. I rejoice with friends sharing drinks, good food, and chocolate cake for dessert. All the while I must keep conscious of expanding inches around the waist. Each of us would do well to observe a holistic philosophy about ourselves, and then extend that same concern to others. Society is a unit, one race of people, the human race, on one small island in space. What we do for the good of others will of necessity reflect back onto our own lives.

We have made many major advancements in this last century and especially in the past forty years — the space age. Yet, our thinking remains very old-fashioned. At times one would think that we are still at the primitive, pre-civilized, even barbaric stage. Our thoughts often revolve around the domination of others. We're still throwing stones as we did in cave-dwelling days. History continues to repeat itself: we still have wars, tribal animosities, and lust for turf. By now we should have moved beyond the point of solving ethnic and national differences by means of war.

The photo of our planet from the moon makes the earth appear as a tiny orb floating free in the dark and hostile void of space. It forces us to see our world in a different perspective. We have such limited, precious space here on our fragile blue globe, yet we still don't give it the tender attention that we should. If we care for the earth it will care for us. If we abuse it, we are ultimately abusing ourselves.

Before we brag too much about progress in civilization we had better define it holistically. If we are truly "space-age" or modern in our thinking, it must be reflected in how we perceive all life on earth. To be truly modern is to think in terms of being one with the earth and with each other. We need to learn anew that it is better to give than to receive. To be modern requires that we do away with the old divisions and resentments and catch the big new view.

Forget about the yesterdays when our world and ancestors were young and inexperienced. Today we are supposed to be smarter. We know there's no future in hatred and divisions. In the holistic picture we realize that when we injure others we only harm ourselves. When rights are violated, society is forced to pass more laws and restrictions. Then we complain about all the restrictions. If basic rights were observed, most of the restrictions could be lifted. That, however, would involve a universal change of attitude, a new way of thinking.

In this world there are so many things which are obviously wrong and out of order. We are foolish to think there is someone in Washington who is going to correct it. The federal government is not going to improve our lives or attitudes. The ones who will do that are ourselves. As said long ago, it will be we, the people. To imagine it any other way is not realistic. If collectively we decide to improve the world it will be improved. If we decide not to, it will continue to deteriorate, for nothing stands still. That's a pure and simple fact, regardless of who is in the White House. I repeat again, each of us is either part of the problem or part of the solution.

Education, communication, and understanding must be established first among people before we will succeed in working for the good of all. When we establish respect for others, true concern will follow.

When we label someone or some race as ignorant or savage then we can more easily discriminate against them without regard for the consequences. If we see these people as persons like ourselves, then we will begin to care. Take the example of the American Indians, once tragically considered ignorant and savage when they were neither. Indians possess deep wisdom and a profound respect for life. They are devoted friends of the land, water and natural resources. They are not savage but reverential, as shown in this beautiful Indian prayer.

"O great spirit, whose voice I hear in the winds and whose breath gives life to all the world, hear me. I am small and weak; I need your strength and wisdom. Let me walk in beauty, and make my eyes ever behold the red and purple sunset. Make my hands respect the things you have made and my ears sharp to hear your voice. Make me wise so that I may understand the things you have taught my people. Let me learn the lessons you have hidden in every leaf and rock. I seek strength, not to be greater than my brother, but to fight my greatest enemy — myself. Make me always ready to come to you with clean hands and straight eyes. So when life fades, as the fading sunset, may my spirit come to you without shame."

It's impossible to undo the evil and injuries which were committed in the past. That's where the virtue of forgiveness must come in. As we have seen time and time again, warring peoples and nations can come to peace and begin again. As the old warning says, "Let us heed the light, otherwise, we'll feel the heat." Our rights are precious but they don't extend indefinitely. There is a limit as to how far we can violate laws and still expect to be protected by them. The same is true when it comes to another person's dignity. Someone once rightly said, "Your right to swing your fist stops at the point my nose begins."

When we cooperate and care we accomplish much good, for what we send into the lives of others eventually comes back into our own.

Someone told me a story about two boys named Fred, both in the 5th grade. One, the smaller, was a major disciplinary problem for the teacher. At the first P.T.A. meeting a very polite lady introduced herself as Fred's mother. Assuming she was the mother of "the other Fred," one of her favorite students, the teacher lavishly praised him, saying what a joy he was to have in class. The following morning, little Fred, the problem child, dashed up to his teacher and threw his arms around her. "Thanks for telling my mother I was a good student and a joy to have in class," he sobbed. Only then did the teacher realize the mistaken identity. She patted his head and wiped a tear from her cheek. From that moment, little Fred began to change — because she had inadvertently given him the hope to think he could change. He became one of her favorite students and ultimately was a joy to have in class.

Realistic change takes time, patience and especially love. It does not happen immediately. We, personally, have all kinds of opportunities to make the world a little better. As Blanchard and Johnson say in *The One Minute Manager*, a good rule to follow is: "Help people reach their full potential. Catch them doing something right." In return we help ourselves, our country, and our world.

As we continue to live in closer proximity with others, it becomes more imperative to show genuine respect and sensitivity. That means we not only stop killing, robbing, injuring, and dominating others. We cease blowing our smoke in other peoples' eyes, blaring our radios in their ears, and refusing to say, "Hello." When we learn how to put together a person who is honest, fair, and caring, the human puzzle will be solved and the world will be together.

14

DARE TO BE INNOVATIVE

An old Arab chieftain one day decided to make his will. He had been a very thoughtful man through his life and now, consistent to his way of thinking, he wished to dispose of his possessions.

His goods, which consisted only of camels, were to be divided up at the time of his death. Half of the camels were to go to his wife. One third would go to his son, his only child. He also remembered his best friend, who was to receive one ninth of his possessions. Some of the camels were sold to pay medical bills in his last days and, at the time of his death, there were 17 camels left. When the will was read, the family did not know how to divide the 17 camels in keeping with the dictates of the will.

In the neighborhood there lived a wise Bedouin, whom the family respected. They, therefore, requested his assistance. The dilemma was explained to him and three days later he came riding his camel to their home, to settle the will. Instead of tying his camel outside, by itself, he placed it in the pen with the other 17. Then the Bedouin sat down with the family.

"There are 18 camels in the lot," he said, "so let's read the will and divide them properly. The wife receives one half: that will be nine. The son receives one third; that is six. Now the good friend of the family gets one ninth; which is two. Thus 9 + 6 + 2 = 17." He asked if the decision fulfilled the wishes of the deceased, and they all agreed the distribution was fair. "Fine," replied the Bedouin. "Now my camel is waiting for me. So if my work is finished, I'll saddle up and be heading home."

Those who are innovative can solve problems and be on their way, while others with less imagination are stalled in the midst of frustration, still struggling for the right answer. To be innovative means to create change and introduce something new. Creative people make life exciting and fill us with a sense of awe. They are the daring ones who love new and different ways of doing their work and finding solutions to difficulties. The spirit of originality inspires inventors, adventurers, trail blazers and all who are pioneers of the new and the untried. They are the heralds of progress who renew the world.

We have many loyal commitments to tradition, for it is the basis of what and where we are at present. Our constitution, business practices, old formulas and court decisions, are all products of tradition. These have set the precedents for making today's decisions. Innovation is not opposed to tradition but it does look in the opposite direction. It's more risky and consequently more challenging.

The reading public was entertained and in-spired in 1973 when Richard Bach's *Jonathan Livingston Seagull* was published. It was the imaginative story of a unique seagull who de-sired to fly fast and low. He practiced, crashed, cried with pain, but tried again — and again and again. Jonathan endured not only his physical hurts but the critical admonitions of his own seagull community. They all warned him to aban-don his ridiculous dreams which were impossible to fulfill.

One night, flying back home, sore and dis-couraged from failures, he agreed his fellow seagulls were right. He agreed, he couldn't fly fast and low. Short, strong wings are required for that feat. The seagulls' wings are meant for soar-ing. They are too long and flimsy for flying fast and low. Jonathan decided to abandon his experi-ments and settle down to be one of the ordinary seagulls. Then, suddenly, a startling revelation hit him. He was flying in the dark. The others had told him seagulls could not fly in the dark. He was doing it, right now! He was doing what they said was impossible. They were wrong! Jonathan immediately realized they could also be wrong about flying fast and low. Immediately, he re-newed his decision to keep trying, for now he was more determined than ever.

Eventually, because of his personal belief and spirit of innovation, Jonathan learned to fly fast and low.

Dilemmas like this face us each and every day. We are told how we ought to think and act and live. But we also need to have the courage at times to innovate. A new invention is not really the discovery of something new. It is simply the bringing together of two or more ideas or elements which had never been joined before. An invention is not a creation, for inventors are not God. They achieve their goals through keen observation and inquisitive minds which continually ask, "What if?"

Everything we have, from light bulbs to airplanes, at one time existed only in a person's mind. The elements of the earth from which they are made were here all along, just waiting to be put together. The materials from which future inventions will come are already present, in some form, just waiting to be combined into something new.

The longing for a new and better way to do something motivates the hearts of artists, poets, and singers, as well as those who came up with a way to vulcanize tires and manufacture automatic dishwashers.

Where did Beethoven find such beautiful melodies? From the notes in an ordinary musical scale which is available to everyone in the world. We can recite the "Do Re Me Fa So La Ti Do" by heart and can even sing it. The person who knows nothing of music understands that, as you move in the scale from left to right you also move from base to soprano. We have heard the musical scale and imitated it thousands of times. Its notes are the building blocks of the musical world. Everything which has been composed has simply depended on the placement of those notes in relationship to each other.

Beethoven is considered by many to be the greatest musical composer of all time. It is said that his music lifts the mortal spirit to the realms of heaven. Others argue that Mozart is superior to Beethoven because he brought the songs of the angels down to earth. Neither of them created the notes; they simply arranged them as they saw best.

Our current English dictionaries by and large contain the same words which Shakespeare and Milton used to express their profoundly beautiful and timeless literature. They were innovators who found new ways and expressive words to make their sentiments and ideas intelligible to others. Once we read their well constructed sentences and expertly chosen combinations, we might wonder why we can't think like that. Maybe we could if we tried. Certainly, we could do better.

The poets and playwrights are especially respectful of each one's unique contribution to the art of finely tuned expressions. William Shakespeare died when John Milton was eight years of age. As a young man, Milton wrote a poem in honor of Shakespeare. He realized that Shakespeare would never need a monument to keep his memory alive for he would live through the words he left the world. Milton wrote:

"What needs my Shakespeare for his
    honored bones,

The labor of an age in piled stones?
Or that his hallowed relics should be hid
Under a starry pointed pyramid?
Dear son of memory, great heir of fame
What need'st thou such weak witness of
   thy name?"

One day I was typing at my computer when
a pencil fell and rolled under the desk. As I tried
to reach it, I unknowingly rested my head on the
keyboard for a few seconds. When I looked at the
screen I saw a strange series of numbers, letters
and symbols and wondered what the odds might
be of printing an intelligent sentence by the acci-
dental touching of the keyboard. Exponential, I
should imagine. The potential for one of the best
books ever written exists right now in my personal computer. I would gladly write it, if only I
knew which keys to touch. We have an overflow
of current technology at our disposal, especially
through the medium of the fascinating computer.
The world is now immersed in new associations,
never before imagined. The times are replete with
many new inventions.

The current "qwerty" typewriter keyboard
arrangement was designed so that the weaker
fingers would do the most work. In this way,
since the original typewriters could only handle
limited speed, the typing would be slower and
the keys would not become jammed. Because
modern day computers don't have this problem
one can type as fast as the computer chips can
process the impulses created by the keys; for this

reason, the Japanese have rearranged the keyboard to let the stronger fingers do most of the work. The new keyboard works with the strength of the fingers, not against them. The computer has revolutionized our society, processing reams of information in a matter of seconds and improving the quality of almost everyone's life. Its potential for good in education, industry and home is virtually unlimited. Would that our spiritual growth might keep pace with the advances being made in some of these innovative areas of science and technology.

There is an urgent need today to reemphasize those values which once made our country great. We have a serious obligation to be more community-minded and less selfish. If moral development and a sense of responsibility toward others continue to erode, society will be seriously impaired.

How can we again discover the golden rule and live by it? The story is told of Felix Pedro who lived in the frigid wilderness of Alaska. One day he was tracking a moose and saw a small golden nugget in the animal's snowy hoof print. Felix realized that the nugget had become dislodged from between the moose's toes, so he began to backtrack. The path led him to a shallow creek which the moose had crossed. There he discovered many more shiny nuggets and that started the Alaskan gold rush.

The desire to find gold back in 1849 brought the "Forty-Niners" rushing to California. "Eureka," a Greek word meaning "I have found it," soon became the state's motto. We may have found the gold in the ground and mined it, but we have not yet found how to extract the golden goodness of the human heart and make it available for the enrichment of humankind. Golden nuggets of wisdom, kindness, fairness and right living are hidden somewhere, waiting to be discovered. When we do, we will experience the greatest gold rush ever.

15

THE SUN WILL SHINE
TOMORROW

An 1857 editorial appeared in the *Boston Globe*, lamenting the sad conditions of the nation. It called the present times "a gloomy moment in the history of our country." The editor could find little security and less hope for the future. "Not in the lifetime of most men," he said, " has there been so much grave and deep apprehension. Never has the future seemed so dismal."

No doubt, many of the readers of the *Boston Globe* in 1857 agreed with the editorial. The future of the United States must have appeared bleak at that time, for the Civil War was only four years away. The question of freedom for the slaves and other issues which caused that war were rapidly dividing the country. Threats and hatred colored the talk of the day and some thought that America's wonderful experiment in democracy was about to end. What the political pundits and editor of the *Globe* could not know was that a President by the name of Abraham Lincoln would keep the nation one and democracy would continue to flourish.

It is our natural tendency to view the evil and negative aspects of situations and envision them as only getting worse. We often can't foresee or hope in those powerful good forces which almost always eventually arise to save what appears to be a certain disaster.

In the midst of tragedy and fear we often wonder if happiness will ever find its way back into our lives. Experience teaches us that it does. We all realize we will not be happy at every stage of life, but we also need to understand that neither will we always be miserable. Annie still walks across the stage and sings: "Tomorrow, tomorrow, I love you tomorrow... The sun will come out tomorrow."

Each generation thinks that their times are the most difficult the world has ever seen. "What," we ask, "must be done to change the tide of events and make the years ahead brighter?" Genuine optimism is often remote. Since the future frequently causes us to fear the worst, we seek consolation in the past.

Affectionately we characterize our yesterdays as "the good ole days." Imagine all "the good ole days" which have taken place since 1857. Ours has been the most eventful and invention-inspired age in the history of the world. All of us now living were born on this side of the Civil War. Headlines of that day, like "The U.S.A. Union Dissolves," never did materialize. The worst was feared but the nation survived and became the world's most powerful country.

Today, again, we see a world full of ills

without apparent solution. The future, however, has a way of bringing pleasant surprises. We should expect them. I recently listened to a song whose lyrics spoke of unrequited love. Its conclusion was filled with hope for tomorrow. "I'll learn to smile after awhile. I'll love again when my heart mends. Only time can heal." Healing, however, doesn't mean our lives return to the way they were. Hurts will change us to some degree even though healing does take place.

Many years ago I bought a colorful plaque on which were written the words: "These are the good old days." Each generation thinks some other time or place was or will be better than today. Thus we need to be reminded of the precious gift each day is to us and to be careful we don't substitute the real beauty around us for some far-off dream.

The German philosopher Hegel built his whole metaphysical system on the three foundations of thesis, antithesis, and synthesis. The thesis is a statement of the current situation — glad, sad, or whatever. The thesis, or current situation, will not endure forever. It exists in tension with its opposite. If, for example, a person is very ill, he exists in tension with the opposite, the antithesis, total good health. The achievement of relative good health is the synthesis. The current synthesis then becomes the next thesis and the progress continues on towards perfection.

We are continually striving for something better than we now have. It is a very part of our nature and bodes well for the future. Every small step ahead extends our long-range goal and we are challenged to go one step further.

Pope John XXIII was an outstanding example of one who saw good, rather than evil, in the future. In a personal letter to a friend in 1932 he wrote: "My approach to life is the same as it has always been, namely, to believe my own eyes, to interpret everything in the best possible light, to take comfort in the good I see around me, rather than to be distraught by the vision of overwhelming evil, and then to look ahead confidently to the future."

He pursued this simple but very optimistic approach to life all his days. Not many thought he would achieve much or be very popular when he was first elected pope. How he surprised the world! Elected at age 76, he served in the papal office less than five years, but his example of love and kindness had a profound impact on the whole world. Indeed, his personal concern for all, his gentleness and praise of others endeared him to everyone he met.

In a book published in 1976, the psychologist Jess Lair writes: "Praise is like sunlight to the warm human spirit. We cannot flower and grow without it." If we want the sun to shine for another, all we need to do is give our praise and encouragement to one we think deserving. It will be the sunshine in that person's soul. Isn't it wonderful to know we don't need to wait for the sun to appear in the sky, for we can make it shine? Sadly the opposite is also true. If the sun is bright in the heavens we still have the power to conceal it from others. Lair restates what we already know: "Most of us are too ready to apply to others the cold wind of criticism; we are somehow reluctant to give others the warm sunshine of praise." The real powers that lift or depress the human spirit are not the literal rays of sun or drops of rain but the kindness we show one to another.

I heard of a third grade class where several boys were continually fighting on the playground. Their teacher talked with them about kindness and forgiveness, directing her remarks especially to Billy and Joey, two of the worst offenders. Their playground conduct improved. Several days later she found this note in Billy's workbook: "Dear Billy, I hate you. Love, Joey."

Perhaps we, like the kids, should not take everything at face value. The "I hate you's" we have uttered against us may not be as fierce as we imagine. In Joey's note to Billy, the love message dominates the hate. Love negates hate for it's stated last.

Clara Barton, the founder of the American Red Cross, once made a statement which can serve as a guiding light on our path. When she was a young lady, someone out of anger and jealousy tried to discredit her reputation with a vicious rumor. Miss Barton was embarrassed and emotionally crushed. She considered abandoning her health-care work because of this evil deed. Eventually she recovered and went on to become an international celebrity in the nursing profession. Many years later, she was having dinner with one of her childhood friends and the early hurt surfaced in their conversation. Her friend, again, lamented how that certain person had tried to ruin her life. Miss Barton didn't answer and appeared not to remember. Her friend reemphasized how deeply Clara had been hurt. "You surely remember that, don't you?" Miss Barton softly smiled and replied: "No, I distinctly remember forgetting that."

In our close proximity with one another in our families, neighborhoods, places of employment, schools and churches, we are bound to encounter hurts and jealousies. If we attempt to keep tab of all of these emotional bruises, we will block the sunshine from our lives. We will be left angry and revenge-filled. Some hurts literally can not ever be forgotten but all of them can be forgiven and dismissed as Clara Barton did. There is no advantage whatsoever in constantly dwelling on past injuries. The sun will shine and opportunities will continue to be present. We must be disposed to enjoy them. If our gloomy attitude blocks out the brightness of daily living, then it might as well be midnight perpetually. There's an old saying: "The person who doesn't read is no more fortunate than the person who can't."

Someone recently wrote an article lamenting the life of the children of wealthy parents. These youngsters, who never need to work for their money, are most unfortunate indeed. Why? Because they are growing up with no knowledge of hardship or failure. Later, when they encounter some setback, they will not know how to cope with the situation. It may seem difficult to accept, but some failure in our lives is necessary. It's the only way we can truly grow. There is no other way to learn the lessons we must be taught. For the person with a purpose, there is actually no such thing as a failure — only another lesson on the way to the success.

Thomas Edison is not remembered for those experiments of his which ended in failure. He is remembered as history's greatest inventor, with more than 1100 patents to his credit. It is reported that he once worked for an extended period of time and tried 10,000 experiments on a storage battery. Each failed. When a friend tried to console him, Edison said, "I've not failed, I just found 10,000 ways it won't work."

If we have a similar kind of driving force within us, we will accomplish difficult tasks and achieve elusive goals too. The sun will shine in our lives if we display tireless determination to meet and conquer complex problems. A noble objective is not enough, though. Many with good intentions fall by the wayside in the face of discouragement. Perseverance is the key to genuine achievement in any field. It's the one essential ingredient to be found in anyone's formula for success.

When perseverance joins forces with discipline, expect to see great results. The poet says:

"For all the hills I've had to climb
  For all the stones which bruised my feet
  For all the sweat, the tears and grime

My heart sings a happy song
For these are the things which made me
    strong."

To be happy, successful and fulfilled, you need not be financially secure, intelligent, strong, or have a glowing personality. Of far greater importance is a confident attitude of mind. What you sincerely think you can do and become, you can.

Some days you won't see the sun and you will need to lean against the wind. It might be very strong and right in your face but you will be victorious because you will be ready. Your courageous achievements will bring you peace of mind. Another sunrise will follow you and you will feel the gentle wind. This time it will be at your back.